A HISTORY OF
THE SABBATH

A HISTORY OF THE SABBATH

by

NATHAN A. BARACK

JONATHAN DAVID

Publishers   New York

A HISTORY OF THE SABBATH
Copyright 1965
by
Nathan A. Barack

Library of Congress Catalogue Card No. 64-8425

ISBN: 978-0-8246-0475-2

PRINTED IN THE UNITED STATES OF AMERICA

TO MY PARENTS
IN WHOSE HOME THE SABBATH
WAS A DAY OF PEACEFUL REST
JOY AND HOLINESS
THIS BOOK IS GRATEFULLY DEDICATED.

"Three testify concerning each other: God, Israel and the Sabbath. God and Israel testify that the Sabbath is a day of repose; Israel and the Sabbath testify that God is One; God and the Sabbath testify that Israel is unique among the nations."

(Midrash, quoted by Tosafot, Haggigah, 3b)

FOREWORD

THE SYSTEM of Judaic regulations known as *mitzvot* (commandments of God) have ever been for the observant Jew a medium of communion with God. Fulfillment of the *mitzvah* should make the adherent aware of, and responsive to, his Creator, Whom he usually addresses prior to the performance of a *mitzvah* with the prescribed formula beginning "Praised be Thou O Lord our God." The performance of the *mitzvah* leads to an awareness of God's Presence and also serves as a reminder of the Jew's membership in a sanctified community, as is evident from the formula words ". . . King of the universe, Who sanctified us by means of His commandments."

The variety of *mitzvot* related to the Sabbath, especially, induces in the practitioner a feeling of closeness to God and to the Jewish community. For Israel's original and unique Sabbath always made Israel distinctive and holy. How the Jewish people felt about their Sabbath throughout the centuries is underscored by Solomon Schechter, in his essay, "The Law and Recent Criticism" (*Studies in Judaism, First Series*):

> . . . we have the testimony of a literature extending over about twenty-five centuries, and including all sorts and conditions of men, scholars, poets and mystics . . . (giving) unanimous evidence in favor of this law, and of bliss and happiness of living, and dying under it. . . . The law of the Sabbath is one of those institutions the strict observance of which was already the object of attack in early New Testament times. Nevertheless . . . we have the prayer of Rabbi Zadok, a younger contemporary of the Apostles, which runs thus: "Through the love with which Thou, O Lord our God, lovest Thy people Israel, and the mercy which Thou hast shown to the children of Thy covenant, Thou hast given unto us this great and holy seventh day."

vii

In this study we endeavor to trace the development of the rabbinic Sabbath from its probable origin in pre-Torah days, through the period of the Talmud (about 500 CE), by which time the character of the Sabbath was essentially established. Some references from later Midrashim are included because they reflect the ideas and spirit, if not the actual words, of those who molded the form of the Sabbath.

We sought to present the history, philosophy, essence and effect of the Sabbath. We realize that our treatment is far from comprehensive. Our work is not, nor is it intended to be, in any way, a *Shulhan Arukh* (a Code of Jewish Law). However, we hope that readers will find in the following pages not only a comparatively systematic presentation of the development and essence of the Sabbath but also a measure of stimulation and inspiration.

Grateful appreciation is expressed to: my father-in-law, Rabbi Joseph D. Astrachan *(alav hashalom)*, Rabbis K. N. Fisher and David Shapiro, Mrs. C. L. Mishkin, my dear father, R. Peretz, the libraries of Congregation Beth El in Sheboygan, the Hillel Foundation of Penn State College and the College of Jewish Studies in Chicago for books used in this study.

We are indebted to Dr. Shraga Abramson, who read the original manuscript, and to Rabbi Alfred J. Kolatch of Jonathan David Publishers, for helpful comments, for suggesting the introductory chapter and title, and for his splendid cooperation.

Finally, to my parents, in whose home the Sabbath was a day of peaceful rest, holiness and joy; to my companion, Lillian, keeper of the sacred and beautiful Sabbath; and to our children, Rivkah, Judie and Sara, to whom the Sabbath is a most welcome, beloved queen, this expression of my own faith is gratefully and lovingly dedicated.

TABLE OF CONTENTS

INTRODUCTION

THE TALMUD, in two interesting and instructive legends, rejects the perfectionist's negation of man's right to existence and spiritual teachings. According to one legend, the angels sought to dissuade God from creating man because he would be deceitful and quarrelsome. God removed the angels, and created man. According to the second legend, the angels argued that man was not worthy of being given the Torah, the precious divine treasure. Emboldened by God, the erstwhile overawed Moses challengingly asked the angels whether they had been enslaved by Pharaoh in Egypt that they needed to be reminded that God is the supreme Lord and Liberator, whether they lived amidst idolaters that they needed to be commanded not to worship idols, whether they labored that they needed a day of rest, etc. (*Sanhedrin,* 38b; *Shabbat,* 88b). The implication is obvious: it is imperfect man, who is involved in a physically and spiritually exhausting struggle for material adequacy and abundance, who is subject to the negative social and spiritual influences in his state and community, and who has need of, and scope for, further development, and therefore for the Torah.

The Torah itself declares that the purpose of the commandments is to maintain and sanctify life. It urges: Keep the laws because they help their practitioner to live (Lev. 18:5); be holy, because I the Lord your God am holy (Lev. 19:2); distinguish between the clean and unclean, for I distinguished you from the idolatrous peoples to be for Me a "kingdom of priests and holy nation" (Lev. 20:25-26; Exod. 19:6). The commandments, our sages commented, were given to purify Israel. Purification or holiness, which is the endeavor to rise to the highest possible level of compassion, righteousness, self-discipline and communion with God, is to be attained by means of all the practices and prohibitions of Judaism, but particularly through the laws of morality, the dietary code and the Sabbath. "Remember the Sabbath Day, to sanctify it (*l'kadsho*)," the fourth commandment teaches. That Judaism regards the Sabbath as primal is shown by the fact that it is the only institution linked with Creation and even with the Creator Himself. It is the culmination of Creation, and receives the Creator's blessing and sanctification. It is the only holy day commanded in the Decalogue. Its importance, dramatized by the miracle of the *manna,* is stressed in a special chapter of Exodus (16). Its divine origin is indicated in the statement, "See that the Lord has given you the Sabbath." It is, like circumcision, a sign of God's covenant, and also, according to Exod. 3:1, a sign of God's santification of Israel.

Judaism has been compared to Jacob's ladder, resting on the earth and reaching to heaven. The Sabbath can be said to be a special model of that ladder. It also rests on the ground, but it reaches to the highest heaven. It inspires its beneficiary to feel that the universe is the work of a purposeful Creator, that human life has meaning and sanctity, that all life must be preserved, and that even animals must be provided with their necessary rest. The Sabbath teaches that physical life, too, is good, and can become meaningful and joyous by making it a medium of communion with God.

Sabbath observance is aimed at freeing man from enslavement to his impulses, and from the routine, tension and lower spiritual level of the work day. The Sabbath incorporates the Judaic insight that man is a psychological as well as a logical being. The Sabbath ban on all non-vital work—which usually is an activity that causes a change in the object or in its visible location—affords complete rest. The prohibition of all dispensable routines and noise tends to set the day apart, and to make it distinctive. This distinctiveness is felt by the Sabbath-keeper, who is thus psychologically prepared for meditation, inspiration and true joy. The discouragement of dispensable routines dates back at least to the days of the Prophets (see Isaiah 58:13). The rabbis, however, systematized and rationalized the prohibitions. To their insight that the Sabbath was instituted to enhance and not to limit living, they added the methodology of interpretation, and clarified the definition of "work" by underlining its motivation. Thus they extended the Torah's dispensations in the case of public sacrifices to other necessary, time-delineated public functions, and to vital individual ones, such as circumcision and the preservation of life.

The Sabbath was a great *pattern of culture* for generations of Jews, and remains so for hundreds of thousands of contemporary Jews. Directly or indirectly it influenced world culture. What meaning has it for the non-Orthodox of today? Is it still relevant, or is it outmoded in our scientifically and technologically transformed world? We believe that the answer depends on what we seek in life. If we seek a meaningful place in a purposeful cosmos, along with values that transcend the material, then the Sabbath is still relevant for us. We shall see this more clearly if we ask ourselves, What meaning has modern life, minus the Sabbath, given man?

David Riesman, author of *The Lonely Crowd,* probably speaks for many other thinkers when he writes in his *Abundance For What?* (p. 307) that "what we fear to face is more than total destruction: it is total meaninglessness." Not more reassuring was Dr. Henry Murray, Harvard psychologist, in an address to the Harvard Chapter of the Phi Beta Kappa.

He said: "Our eyes and ears are incessantly bombarded by a mythology that breeds greed, envy, pride, lust and violence . . . a mythology that is (not) sufficient to the claim of head and heart. . . ." (*Fate of Man*, p.14). Dr. Murray asked for the development of a new "mythology," comparable in scope and influence to that of the Bible—a goal we regard as unnecessary . . . and unattainable!

In fact, a mythology similar to the one suggested by Dr. Murray has been tried, and found wanting. Marxists profess their system to be based on the principles of science and justice. Yet, this alleged union of science and justice, with its vast literature, failed to produce enduring meaning in the country of its greatest success, as George Bailey points out in an article in *The Reporter* (July 16, 1964). On the basis of his observations, and interviews with *non-religious* Russians, Bailey concluded that "the lack of sanctuary in Soviet society has prompted a search for substitute sanctuaries." A Muscovite remarked, "There is no essential dignity in the Soviet system." Man's lack of fulfillment is not peculiar only to the Russian Marxist philosophy, as is evident from an article entitled, "Kafka East, Kafka West," by Harvey Cox, in *The Commonweal* (Sept. 4, 1964). The author makes these significant statements: "He (Kafka) realized decades before the many young Marxist theoreticians who have learned it, that man's alienation from himself and his neighbor points to a dimension of existence which far transcends his participation in the economic and political institutions of human society. . . . It is the residue of alienation, still persistently present in socialist societies, which puzzles honest Marxist thinkers today." A feeling of disillusionment and alienation also exists in Israel's non-religious *kibbutzim*, although these were founded by democratic seekers of a non-urbanized, cooperative way of life.

Bailey comments: "The concerted anti-Semitic campaign

in the Soviet Union is always—directly or indirectly—connected with the Jew's religion, and the drive against the Jew is the spearhead of the general drive to destroy the Judeo-Christian ethic. Soviet Communists regard the Jew as the religious archetype, Judaism as the primordial religion." In this the Communists of Russia betray their fear that their atheistic, scientific socialism is really inferior to Judaism, which not only teaches social justice and the sanctity of the individual life, but also presents a meaningful philosophy of life with a system of creative self-discipline, especially as embodied in the Sabbath.

Today, no artificially-developed mythology will serve to overcome the feeling of alienation experienced by modern thinking individuals, nor will it sway the less reflective to turn from their various forms of escapism. One cannot, by fiat, fabricate a creed that will endure, and that will capture the hearts and minds of people. Only a faith reaching higher than mankind, and one with a sanctified pattern of self-discipline, can satisfy and endure.

The relevance of the Sabbath for modern man is necessarily related to the basic belief in a Creator Who cares for His creatures. Consequently, a brief statement about the validity of this belief is necessary. Basically, there are three causes for modern man's turning from a meaningful belief in God: 1) science, 2) human suffering and 3) materialism. The first does not loom as large as it did when science first began to challenge the ideas of the acknowledged religious leaders. Today, it is recognized that the function of science is not to deal with ultimate values but mainly with processes. The expanding discoveries of the natural processes make it more evident that the universe is the product of a marvellous Intelligence. The Deists thought that human affairs were too unimportant for the infinite Creator of the universe. Today we conceive the Infinite as encompassing every particle of existence, including, of course, man, whose heart and mind are not only part of the natural universe, but also probably its highest level of evolution.

Today, we realize that the satisfactions provided by materialistic goals cannot satisfy man's spirit. They can drug him into forgetting higher values, but with the inevitable re-awakening come disillusionment, frustration and emptiness.

The questions which are asked concerning human suffering remain unanswered and disturbing to the open-minded atheist, too. However, rather than move us to reject that outlook which provides most meaning to life, such questions should lead us to a sense of humility about the inadequacy of our minds and hearts, and about the imperfection of man's identification with the total cosmic purpose. We are morally obligated to transcend our human ambitions and fears, in order to involve ourselves far beyond our custom in the endeavor to complete Creation and to perfect the world.

Finally, is the traditional Sabbath observance compatible with modern technology? We believe not only that it is compatible, but also that it is needed today even more than when when social life was far more simple. Modern man is subject to constant pressures and tensions. Modern mechanization patterns of mass living tend to dehumanize and diminish him. He needs to change his weekly routine and to spend more time with his family and friends in wholesome fellowship and exchange of ideas. He needs to bring dignity and sanctity into his life. Moreover, automation affords him more leisure and opportunity for intellectual and spiritual growth. The traditional Sabbath offers all that. Of course, inherent in modern society are essential functions that must continue through the week. As a careful perusal of the following pages will show, such modifications of the

Sabbath rest are within the context of the traditional Sabbath—as long as real necessity and not mere convenience
determines the dispensation.

The Judaic Sabbath is a precious gift, the product of
both religious genius and divine guidance, and its great
benefits for the individual and for society will yet, it may
be hoped, be rediscovered by modern man.

A HISTORY OF
THE SABBATH

CHAPTER I

The Sabbath From Creation to Ezra

(As viewed by biblical and midrashic authors)

IN THE BOOK OF GENESIS (2:1-3) we read: "The heavens and the earth, and all their hosts, were completed. On the seventh day God completed His work which He had made, and He rested on the seventh day from all His work which He had made. God blessed the seventh day, and He hallowed it, because on it He rested from all His work which He created to do."

The Torah's statement that God completed His work on the seventh day seems to contradict the statement following it, that He rested on the seventh day which, of course, is the very basis of the Sabbath. Therefore, the seventy-two elders who translated the Torah into Greek for King Ptolemy of Egypt changed the verse to read, "On the sixth day God completed His work. . . ." The rabbis, however, found the traditional reading compatible with the rest of the passage, for to them creation was completed with the Sabbath. "What was the world lacking at the end of the sixth day?" the Midrash asks, and answers, "Rest, Sabbath . . . and this was the completion on the seventh day." According to Gniva the six days of creation were only accessory to the seventh day, for "this is comparable to a King who made himself a canopy . . . but lacked a bride. . . ." According to the Sages, the Sabbath was the climax of creation, for "it is analogous to

1

a King who made himself a ring which was lacking a seal. Likewise, what was the world lacking? The Sabbath!" Some rabbis, however, probably concerned with the literal meaning of the difficult verse, accepted Rabbi Simon bar Yohai's interpretation that God, who knows time precisely, extended His creation into the Sabbath by a hairbreadth, and thus, completed His work at the start of the seventh day.[1] Creation was thus, according to all, culminated with the hebdomadal or weekly Sabbath.[2]

The Torah does not state, nor even hint, that the Patriarchs kept the Sabbath. In rabbinic literature, however, we find differing views on the subject. According to Rabbi Yose ben Halaphta, Abraham did not observe the Sabbath, but Jacob did; and he even established *t'humei Shabbat,* the 2000 cubits limit within which a person may walk beyond the city, or his resting place outside a city, on the Sabbath. Another rabbi declared that Abraham knew, and fulfilled, all the Sabbath laws.[3] Joseph, too, according to Rabbi Yohanan, kept the Sabbath; and God rewarded him by allowing his descendant, the Prince of the Tribe of Ephraim, to offer his sacrifice on the Sabbath, when the Tabernacle was dedicated in the desert.[4]

Some rabbis believed that the Israelites in Egypt were able to rest on the Sabbath through the intercession of Moses. Moses figured back to the creation of the world, and ascertained the day of the Sabbath.[5] He went to Pharaoh, and said, "A slave who does not rest one day a week cannot live, and your slaves, too, will die if you do not give them a weekly day of rest." Pharaoh granted Moses' request; and Moses established the Sabbath as the day of rest.[6] In the desert, Moses reminded the Israelites, "See that the Lord gave (in the past) you the Sabbath," in Egypt.[7] It was on the Sabbath that the Children of Israel began to read and enjoy the scrolls which recorded God's promise to redeem them. Later on when Moses came to Pharaoh and demanded, "Let us go to sacrifice to our God" (Exod. 5:8), the king blamed the Sabbath rest of the Israelites as having encouraged new demands, and therefore commanded his taskmasters to abolish the Sabbath rest, and to "occupy the people with more burdensome work."[8] Another midrashic view is that the Israelites received the command to keep the Sabbath in Marah, as is implied by the Torah when it states that "there (at Marah) the Lord made a statute and law for the people. . . ." (Exod. 15:26).[9]

The Sabbath was commanded (for the first time, according to the general rabbinic view), and its importance was dramatically conveyed, in the Desert of Sin, where the Israelites arrived on the fifteenth day of the second month of their departure from Egypt.[10] They soon complained about the lack of food, and God told Moses that He would rain down bread from the sky. The people were to gather it, a day's portion every day, except on the sixth day when "that which they will bring in shall be twice as much as that they gather daily." In the evening, as Moses had foretold, "quails came up and covered the camp"; and in the morning, after the dew evaporated, "there was on the surface of the wilderness a fine, scaly substance" which, as Moses explained, was the bread promised by God. The Children of Israel gathered the *manna*, as they called the food. Some gathered more, some, less; but, miraculously, when they measured what they had gathered, all had just enough for their needs (an *omer* per person). Moses commanded that no one leave any *manna* from one day to the next. When certain Israelites disobeyed and left some *manna* until the following morning, it became wormy and foul; and Moses was angry.[11]

On the sixth day the Israelites discovered that what they had gathered was twice the daily quantity.[12] Their leaders reported this remarkable phenomenon to Moses. He then proclaimed God's command that they keep the following, seventh, day as "a Sabbath, holy unto the Lord." He urged them, "Bake what you need to bake and cook what you need to cook, and that which is left put aside for tomorrow." This time what was left until the next day did not spoil.

The Israelites were commanded by Moses not to try to gather any *manna* on the seventh day, "for today is a Sabbath unto the Lord; today you shall not find it in the field." Some Israelites, however, did go out to gather, but found no *manna*. God then told Moses: " 'Until when will you refuse to keep My commandments and My teachings? See that the Lord has given you the Sabbath; therefore, He gives you on the sixth day bread for two days. Let every man stay in his place and not go out from it on the seventh day.' And the Children of Israel rested on the seventh day." (Exod. 16).

Three weeks after the Sabbath was dramatically promulgated by means of the *manna* miracles, God gave the Israelites the Decalogue, in which He again commanded the keeping of the Sabbath. The Sabbath commandment was fourth, being the bridge between the first three (which concern man's relationship to God) and the last six (which concern man's relationship to his neighbor). The wording of the fourth commandment differs in its Exodus version from that in Deuteronomy. In Exodus it reads:

> *Remember* the Sabbath day to keep it holy. Six days you shall labor, and do all your work; but the seventh day is a Sabbath to the Lord your God. On it do not do any work, neither you nor your son nor your daughter nor your male servant nor your female servant nor your cattle nor your alien residing within your gates. For in six days the Lord made the heavens and the earth, the

sea and all within them; and He rested on the seventh day. Therefore, the Lord blessed the day of the Sabbath, and sanctified it. (20:8-11)

In Deuteronomy the fourth commandment reads:

Be watchful to sanctify the Sabbath Day, as the Lord your God commanded you. . . . Do not do any work . . . nor your ox nor your donkey . . . that your male and female servants may rest as well as you. And you shall remember that you were a servant in the Land of Egypt, and the Lord your God brought you out from there by a mighty hand and by an outstretched arm; therefore, the Lord your God commanded you to practice the Sabbath. (5:12-15)

The two versions contain conceptual as well as linguistic differences, but it is mainly the latter that traditionalist authors tried to reconcile. They regarded the Exodus version as the commandments engraved on the first Tablets, given before the making of the Golden Calf, and the Deuteronomy version as the commandments Moses inscribed on the second Tablets, after he broke the first. The differences were explained variously. According to the *Mekhilta, Zakhor* (the Hebrew word beginning the fourth commandment in Exodus) and *Shamor* (the Hebrew word beginning the fourth commandment in Deuteronomy) were both expressed in one utterance, as were "Everyone who desecrates it (the Sabbath) shall be put to death" and "On the Sabbath day two he-goats (should be offered) . . ." although the latter involved desecrations which ordinarily entailed the death penalty.[13] However, Rabbi Shimeon ben Lakish asserts that the opening words of the two versions of the fourth commandment did indeed differ, and for a good reason. "This is comparable," he explains, "to a king who sent his son to the store with a bottle and a coin (to make a purchase). The boy, however, broke the bottle and lost the coin. The father pinched the boy's ear and pulled his hair, and then gave him another bottle and coin, with the admonition, 'Be careful that you do not lose these as you lost the others.' Likewise, because the Israelites caused Moses to break the first Tablets in which it was writen *Zakhor* (Remember), God gave them the second Tablets in which He wrote, *Shamor* (meaning, keep or be watchful)."[14]

The Sabbath, according to the two versions of the Decalogue, was given to remind us that God created the world and to grant all, including servants and beasts of burden, a day of rest. A third reason is that the Sabbath is a sign of God's sanctification of Israel, as we read in Exodus:

> . . . keep My Sabbaths, for it is a sign between Me and you, for your generations, that you may know that I the Lord sanctify you . . . an eternal covenant. It is a sign between Me and the Children of Israel forever; for in six days the Lord made the heavens and the earth, and on the seventh day He ceased (from work) and rested. (31:12-17).[15]

The Torah specifies what constitutes work on the Sabbath only in a few instances. Plowing and reaping (Exod. 34:21), making a fire (Exod. 35:3) and leaving one's domain (Exod. 16:29) are specifically forbidden. The *Mekhilta* interprets the last listed prohibition to mean that a man may not carry anything, aside from the garments and ornaments he wears, from his property to a public domain, nor may he carry in a public domain four cubits, nor walk 2000 cubits outside his city (or his established place of rest outside a city).[16] The ban on cooking and baking is implied (Exod. 15:23), as interpreted by Onkelos, Rashi and Nahmanides. Numbers 15:32-36 tells about a death penalty (by stoning) meted out to a man who gathered wood on the Sabbath.

However, according to one rabbi, the man was stoned because he carried four cubits in the public domain. According to another rabbi, he was convicted because he plucked
plants on the Sabbath. A third rabbi says he was condemned
because he tied stalks of grain into sheaves.[17] Tradition, as
recorded in the Mishna, lists 39 categories of work forbidden
by the Torah.

The need to offer a sacrifice (in cases of unwitting transgressions) and the death penalty applied only to desecrations
forbidden by the Torah.[18] Trading on the Sabbath, for instance, is mentioned by Amos (8:4-5) but is not implied in
the Torah. It is, therefore, only a rabbinic prohibition.[19]

The death penalty was meted out only if the culprit was
specifically warned by two witnesses. According to the rabbis,
the witnesses who discovered the woodgetter (*mekoshesh*)
warned him that if he persisted in his desecration he would
merit death.[20]

The Tabernacle was not constructed on the Sabbath; but
the two daily *Tamid* sacrifices, the additional Sabbath sacrifice (*Musaph*), and the offering of the Prince of the Tribe of
Ephraim, when the Tabernacle was dedicated, were all
brought on the Sabbath.[21]

According to a rabbinic tradition, Moses instituted the
reading from the Torah on the Sabbath, festivals and new
moon.[22] The later prophets added Torah readings on Mondays and Thursdays, so that three consecutive days should
not pass without Torah instruction. Ezra increased the established three verses read (for Kohanim, Levites and Israelites)
to a minimum of ten verses (for the quorum of ten), to be
read by three persons. He also instituted the following pro-
cedures: the reading of the Torah at Sabbath *Minha;* the
washing of garments on Thursday (in honor of the Sabbath); the eating of garlic on Friday (for fruitfulness, for
Friday night was a time for co-habitation).[23]

CHAPTER II

Origin and Development of the Sabbath

1. Origin

THE SABBATH is one of the greatest institutions evolved by man, and its influence on our civilization has been most profound; therefore, it is not surprising that its origin has evoked great intellectual curiosity. Scholarly speculation has also concerned itself with its name and hebdomadal (weekly) recurrence.

Rest days are observed by primitive agriculturalists, but are unknown among nomadic pastoral tribes, for "a sabbath involves a settled life, a fairly developed social organization and some calendar system."[1]

Buddhists observe the first, eighth, fifteenth and twenty-second of the month as days of fasting.[2] The Babylonians regarded the seventh, fourteenth, twenty-first and twenty-eighth days as days of ill omen.[3] On the Babylonian evil days, "the shepherd of the great tribes shall not eat salted meat cooked over the embers; he shall not change his holy clothing; he shall not be clothed in white; he shall not offer a sacrifice. The king shall not ride in a chariot; he shall not talk victoriously. The seer shall not make a declaration with regard to a sacred place. The physician shall not touch a sick man. It is not suitable to make a wish." These rules are quoted by T. G. Pinches from a Babylonian tablet; and he adds that the Babylonian day began in the evening, at sunset, "as with the Jews."[4] To the Romans, the seventh day, the Day of Saturnus, was an evil day.[5]

The Babylonians used to call the day of the full moon, which was set aside for the worship of the moon and related gods, as *Shappatu.* Is there any connection between it and the Sabbath? Scholars differ in their answers. Some find significance in the similarity of the names, in the hebdomadal occurrence of the Sabbath, and in the fact that the Bible seems to associate it with the new moon.[6] "The Sabbath," says William Rainey Harper, "is mentioned often with the new moon, and seems to have been closely connected with it, probably coming every seventh day after. In the course of time (the Sabbath) became more important than the new moon, and recurrence every seventh day became independent of the new moon."[7] Some scholars agree with Solomon Goldman that "despite endless research (it is) still an open question . . . whether there is any relation at all, and what it is, between the Jewish Sabbath and . . . a Babylonian lunar festival."[8] Dr. Jacob Lauterbach expresses the viewpoint of several leading scholars when he writes, "The Babylonian 'Shabbatu' connected with, and determined by the phases of the moon, while it may have some superficial resemblance to the Jewish Sabbath, was in reality of an entirely different character."[9] "The hebdomadal Sabbath," writes George Foote Moore, "was in fact exclusively Jewish; nothing corresponding to it existed in the Greek and Roman world, nor so far as is known, elsewhere in antiquity."[10] Professor Bart points out that whereas the Babylonian days of rest were evil days, the Jewish Sabbath was always a day of joy, blessed by God; the Jews were forbidden to trade on the Sabbath or even gather wood, whereas the Babylonians could do these things. Professor Bart asserts that even the name is not Babylonian in origin for *Shappatu* did not apply to the seventh, fourteenth, twenty-first and twenty-eighth of the month; these days are not so designated, even once, on Babylonian tablet inscriptions. The same scholar also emphasizes the fact that the Bible does not mention that Israel's neighbors kept the Sabbath, as it mentions that the Ishmaelites observed circumcision (Gen. 17:11).[11] This latter point is also stressed, directly or indirectly, by Dr. William Albright and I. Abrahams. Dr. Albright writes: "Isaiah (who, according to non-Orthodox scholars, lived in Babylonia) welcomes converts (56:3), but in the same chapter mentions the Sabbath as distinctive of Jews."[12] Abrahams writes: "It is still far from clear whether or not the Hebrew Sabbath was a derivative from Babylonia. But whatever its origin, it became one of the most specifically Hebraic institutions. So much was this the case, that the day was regarded as a symbol of the close relationship between Israel and God."[13]

The essentially traditionalist scholar Professor U. Cassuto writes:

In Exodus 16:23, the Sabbath, including the prohibition of labor, is treated as already known, although the Children of Israel had not yet received the Ten Commandments.[14] In the epic tradition of Mesopotamia, which was surely known to the patriarchs from the time of their residence there, every important achievement is pictured as taking place during a span of six days, reaching its completion or perfection, or a new and important phase, on the seventh day. And Jewish tradition had already described creation as having taken place during six days, with the seventh day as one of rest. On the basis of this knowledge, the Children of Israel were able to understand what is said here regarding the distinction between the seventh day and the six days. . . .

In Mesopotamia, the place of origin of the patriarchs,[15] a definite day of the month was known as 'Shabbatu'.

Hence, the name was already known to the Children of Israel, although the character of the Mesopotamian Shabbatu was very different from Israel's Sabbath.[16]

Dr. Cassuto points out the basic differences between the Jewish Sabbath and the Babylonian *Shabbatu,* in the following quotation:

The Jewish Sabbath, apparently, was established in opposition to the Mesopotamian philosophy. Its nature is a complete innovation. It does not depend on the phases of the moon, but comes regularly every seventh day. It is not a day set aside for the worship of heavenly bodies, but of the Creator of the world. It is not a day of self-denial and ill omen but of blessing and rest. The prohibition of work is not because it will not succeed, but because on this day man rises above the daily need to work for a livelihood, becoming godly, for God, too, rested after six days of work. The Jewish Sabbath took on a new, and absolutely original and lofty form. Therefore, the Torah commands, "Remember the Sabbath day," which you already know, but consecrate it, and raise it above the accepted level.[17]

Jewish tradition seems to bear out Professor Cassuto's view. Legend pictures Abraham as one who temporarily accepted and then rejected Babylonian idolatry. This means that the Babylonian idolatrous view and way of life were the material on which Abraham reflected. He probably considered, and eventually rejected, the Babylonian view and observance of the ill-fated rest days. Preoccupied with more elementary and individual concepts, he was unable to transform the *Shabbatu* into the kind of institution that the Sabbath later became. Therefore, there is no mention in the Torah that the patriarchs kept the Sabbath. However, the modification of the *Shabbatu* may have started in Abraham's day, and its evolution may have been carried forward by Abraham's descendants, especially by Jacob and his family.[18]

The idea of a Sabbath, especially as modified by the patriarchs, was probably transmitted to the Israelites, or to the Tribe of Levi. Later on Moses may have gone to Pharaoh, and requested, in accordance with the midrashic tradition, a day of rest for the Israelite slaves.[19] The primary importance of the Sabbath as a day of rest for all, including servants and beasts of burden, is evident from its repeated emphasis in the Torah (Exod. 20:10, 23:12; and Deut. 5:14-15).[20] However, probably from the very beginning Moses envisioned the liberation in spiritual as well as in physical terms.[21] It is also probable that even before the Exodus, or shortly after (at Marah, for instance, as suggested by some rabbis) Moses redefined the purpose of the Sabbath as a day dedicated to God. Therefore, when the Decalogue was given, the Sabbath commandment began, *"Remember* the day of the Sabbath, to sanctify it,"* for its essence was already known to the Israelites.

During the days of the First Commonwealth the Sabbath was observed as a national day of rest. Even in the idolatrous Kingdom of Israel it was kept, as can be seen from the following prophecies of Amos and Hosea: "And I will bring to an end all her mirth, her festivals, her new moons, her Sabbaths and all her special occasions" (Hosea 2:13). "Hear this, you who seek to destroy the country's needy and poor saying, 'When will the new moon pass that we may sell grain, and the Sabbath that we may offer corn for sale?'" (Amos 8:45). That Judah kept the Sabbath as a national institution even in her unrighteous days can be seen from Isaiah's words (1:13): "Bring no more vain offering; your incense is an abomination to Me; your calling of solemn assemblies on the new moon and Sabbath, I cannot bear. . . ." Because the Sabbath was a nationally-accepted institution and because ritual was regarded by them a way to God and to righteous living, the prophets generally did not deem it advisable to urge Sabbath observance by unrighteous people. (Similarly they did not emphasize prayer, in which they surely believed and found inspiration, but denounced it when unaccompanied by righteous living.) To the prophets it was only when the belief in a universal and just Creator became a living inspiration, that the Sabbath would begin to fulfill its purpose as a day of rest for servants too, as well as a reminder of God as Creator.

The prophets probably stressed the Sabbath as a day of rest for the needy, as can be inferred from the reason for the Sabbath given in the Decalogue of Deuteronomy, a book strongly influenced by the prophets. Jeremiah specifically taught this (chapter 17), declaring in the name of God:

> Carry no load from your homes on the day of the Sabbath, and do no work. Sanctify the Sabbath, as I commanded your fathers. . . . If you will listen to Me, and you will not bring burdens on the Sabbath through the gates of the city, and you will sanctify the Sabbath by not doing any work, then through the gates of this city will enter kings and princes who will sit on the throne of David; and this city will be inhabited forever. . . .[22]

During the Babylonian exile the Jews began to drift away from their national institutions, including the Sabbath. Ezekiel, and the exilic Isaiah, therefore, stressed the Sabbath as a sign of God's covenant with Israel, and as a means of making Israel distinct and holy. Ezekiel proclaimed, in the name of God:

> I brought them out of the Land of Egypt and brought them to the desert. I gave them My statutes . . . which a man shall follow and live by. Also My Sabbaths I gave unto them, to know that I the Lord sanctify them. But

> the Children of Israel rebelled against Me in the desert,
> and did not follow My decrees. . . . They desecrated My
> Sabbaths. . . . And it shall be for a sign between Me and
> you, to know that I am the Lord your God. (Ezekiel,
> ch. 20; see also 23:39; 44:24; 45:17; 46:1-5).[23]

Writes Salo Baron:

> The Sabbath now gained a prominence which it never
> had before. To be sure, the institution as such seems
> to belong to the most ancient in Israel. Its inclusion in
> the Decalogue, as the only festival, immediately after
> the commandment pertaining to the unity of God,
> makes it probable that it reaches back to the Mosaic
> age. . . . From the beginning, its social element, the idea
> of rest for the worker, was prominent. . . . After the
> national disaster, however, the evanescent social conflict
> gave way to the national tendency toward segregation
> and holiness. But whether primarily social or religious,
> whether rooted in national or cosmic history, the day
> became the paramount national institution, especially
> for those in the dispersion.[24]

Elsewhere Baron writes that Ezekiel "drew the distinction
between Jew and Gentile on precisely this basis of Sabbath
observance." That the Sabbath became very dear to the
Babylonian captives can be inferred also from the fact that
Shabbatai became the most familiar of the new Hebrew
names adopted by the exiles.[25]

The post-exilic Isaiah, living probably during the days
of Cyrus, when the Jewish people and Judaism attained
unprecedented popularity, urged Sabbath observance not
only by Jews but also by converts, as is evident from his
following words:

> If you will keep from going about your business on the
> Sabbath. . . . My holy day . . . if you will call the Sab-
> bath a delight . . . then I shall cause you to ride on the

high places of the earth. . . . (58:13-14). Observe justice,
and do righteousness. . . . Happy is the man . . . that
keeps the Sabbath from profaning it. . . . And let not
the foreign member, who attached himself to the Lord,
saying, 'The Lord will surely separate me from His
people' . . . for thus said the Lord . . . the non-Jewish
members, that joined themselves to the Lord, to serve
Him and to love the name of the Lord, to be His servants, who keep the Sabbath from desecrating it, and
who keep My covenant, I shall bring them to My holy
mountain, and I will cause them to rejoice in My house
of prayer . . . for My house shall be called a house of
prayer for all peoples. . . . (56:1-7). And it shall be that
from one new moon to another, and from one Sabbath
to another, all flesh will come to worship before Me
(66:23).

Under Ezekiel's leadership the Sabbath became closely
associated with congregational worship.[26] Ezekiel and his
followers were master builders, for they succeeded in getting
the Jewish community in Babylonia to keep the Sabbath
rigorously.[27] In that community grew up Nehemiah, who,
during his terms as governor of Jerusalem, devoted his great
talents and energy to fortify Jerusalem and bring social re-
form, and also strengthen observance of the Sabbath. In
chapter ten of his book he writes that the returned exiles had
signed a covenant to follow the Torah of Moses, "and not
to buy the wares and grain brought on the Sabbath and holy
days by the surrounding peoples." This covenant was broken
after his return to Persia. Nehemiah describes the deplor-
able situation he discovered upon his second tour in Judah:

In those days I saw in Judah people treading the wine
presses on the Sabbath, and bringing in heaps of grain
loaded on donkeys, also wine grapes, figs and all kinds
of burdens, which they brought to Jerusalem on the day
of the Sabbath. . . . I quarreled with the nobles of Judah,

and said to them, "What is this evil thing you are doing, desecrating the Sabbath day? Is not this what your fathers did? And God brought on us all this evil, and on this city. And you are bringing more wrath on Israel, by desecrating the Sabbath". . . . On the eve of the Sabbath, when the evening shadows began to fall upon the gates of Jerusalem, I ordered the gates shut . . . until after the Sabbath. I placed a few of my boys in charge of the gates, so that none was permitted to bring in a load on the Sabbath day. . . . (Nehemiah 13:15-22).

Nehemiah was an effective, practical leader who dealt with the urgent problems of his day. A more famous contemporary, Ezra the Scribe, teacher and editor, played a decisive role in the development of Judaism, and hence of the Sabbath. It was under Ezra's inspired, intellectual leadership that the framework of the rabbinic Sabbath began to rise.

2. Development of the Sabbath

The Sabbath evolved, organically, during the millennium beginning with the Mosaic period, from a weekly day of rest into a religio-national institution, with a definite mode of observance and worship. Already during the days of the prophets it was common practice to abstain from work and trade and to visit the Temple or a prophet on the Sabbath. The fall of the First Temple, and particularly the Babylonian exile, threatened the survival of the Jewish nation and, inevitably, of the Sabbath. Fortunately, because of the endeavors of Ezekiel and his disciples, the Sabbath was not only preserved but became a most symbolic and distinguishing institution of the Jews. When Ezra and Nehemiah, products of the revitalized Babylonian community, came to restored Judah, they found disorganization, confusion and neglect in the religious life of the community. Nehemiah proceeded to purify the family, to free the oppressed, to re-sanctify the Sabbath and to fortify Jerusalem. Ezra the Scribe and his associates, the Men of the Great Assembly, were no longer content with temporary reforms, exhortations, or even unsystematized religious decisions reached on the basis of custom or personal insight, as was common with the priests and prophets. They began to guide the people, and to meet religious contingencies through a systematic and continuous interpretation of relevant Torah passages. When necessary, in order to advance the general goal of holiness and spiritual peoplehood, they also deliberately instituted new rules and reforms. They applied a progressive approach also to the Sabbath, a basic institution of Judaism.

Nehemiah tells us how he enforced certain Sabbath pro-hibitions which, no doubt, had become part of the routine observance of Babylonian Jewry. According to the Talmud, he and Ezra went beyond the accepted restrictions. "At first," the Tosephta states, "only three vessels were permitted to be handled on the Sabbath, a knife for fig cakes, a soup ladle and a small table knife. More were permitted gradu-ally, until only a large saw and the pin of the plow were forbidden."[28] The Gemara explains that the restrictions were enacted during the days of Ezra and Nehemiah, when the people were lax in their Sabbath observance, and "hedges" to the Torah had to be constructed.[29] Whether or not the talmudic tradition is right in ascribing these *particular* re-strictions to the two great reformers, it is surely right in ascribing to Ezra and his school the planning of measures devised to preserve and advance the Sabbath.

The systematic interpretation of the Torah and tradition as developed by Ezra and his associates was carried forward by the Soferim. Like their great teacher, "they laid down lines of progress which were to stretch down the centuries; but neither he nor they were making a new beginning."[30]

Ezra and the Soferim saved the Torah from "becoming a closed revelation to an open one. . . . This is the real significance of the unwritten Torah, and its introduction beside the written text."[31]

The tradition of systematic interpretation was continued by the Pharisees who endeavored to raise and regularize ethical-religious standards by embodying them in the *halakhah* (regulated way of life), which was derived from the literal or implied meaning of the Torah. According to Herford, the Pharisee first sought to answer the question, "How shall God be truly served in this present world"?[32] However, the Pharisee felt that not only was he personally and directly accountable to God as an isolated human being in the presence of his Maker, but also that he was one of a community whose ideals of service he shared and whom he could either help or hinder in pursuing these ideals.[33] Hence, *halakhah* became the way of life of those eager to serve God and establish and safeguard the Jewish people as a sanctified community.

The strict adherence to the Sabbath which the Men of the Great Assembly and the Soferim succeeded in establishing, allowed the Pharisee teachers to remove some of the temporary "hedges," as implied in the Tosephta. Rigorous laws were reinterpreted in response to urgent circumstances. However, these alleviations came only after their need or wisdom was clearly established. Thus, the people of Jerusalem refused to defend their city on the Sabbath, when it was besieged by Ptolemy I, about the year 320 B.C.E.[34] About a century and a half later, when Antiochus Epiphanes sought to supress the observance of the Sabbath, the Jews still refused to fight, or even to defend their lives on the Sabbath. It was then that the leader of the age, Mattathias, ruled that it is permissible to desecrate the Sabbath in self-defense. His reason for the ruling, characteristic of Judaism,

was: "If we follow their (those who refused to defend themselves on the Sabbath) example, and refuse to fight on the
Sabbath even for our lives and laws, then the heathen will
quickly root us out of the earth." He and his associates then
decreed, "Whoever shall come to battle with us on the Sabbath day, we will fight against him. . . ."[35]

The Maccabean decision to fight on the Sabbath in self-
defense was not applied to areas of non-combat, at least for
another century. Thus, when Pompey's army failed in their
attempt to take the Temple, because the Jews from their
superior position used all possible means to repel the enemy,
Pompey cunningly utilized the Sabbath day to fill in a valley
to the north of the Temple, with no interference from the
Jews. However, he kept his soldiers from actual fighting, for
the Jews would have fought back on the Sabbath. After they
had raised an embankment, the Romans erected a high
tower, and by means of their battering engines sought to
knock down the wall.[36]

Several other restrictions mentioned in the *Book of Jubilees* and *Fragments of a Zadokite Work* were later removed.
The *Book of Jubilees* forbids war on the Sabbath, and decrees death for travelling on the Sabbath or for cohabitation,
and for several activities which were later forbidden only by
rabbinic decree.[37] In *Fragments of a Zadokite Work*, a man
is forbidden to lend anything to his neighbor on the Sabbath; a guest who arrived after the Sabbath has started may
not eat food prepared by others; the cover of a vessel may
not be opened on the Sabbath if it is pasted on; a father
may not carry his infant child out of, or into, a house; an
animal may not be raised out of a pit into which it had
fallen; nor may one "bring up by a ladder or cord or instrument another person who had fallen into a place of water."[38]

Sabbath laws, like other Judaic regulations, were more
authoritatively established and universalized after the setting

up of the religious Sanhedrin, and especially after Hillel and Shammai became its heads.[39] A decision favored by the majority of the members of the *Beit Din* (court) became the law or sanctioned way (*halakhah*).[40] Such decisions became binding on the dissenting judges, too, as is shown in the moving story the Mishna tells about Akaviah ben Mahallalel. He had persisted in his dissent against the majority decision, even after his colleagues had promised to choose him head of the court if he would change his opinion, because, he declared, "It is better for me to be regarded a fool all my life than to be, even if only for one hour, a *rasha* in the presence of God (that is, one who acts against his own conscience and causes people to think that he changed his opinion to gain a coveted office)." His colleagues finally excommunicated him, but Akaviah did not abandon his view. However, before he died, he requested his son to accept the majority opinion. To his son's question, "Why did *you* persist in your opinion?" he answered that he, like his colleagues, received his ideas from a *group* of teachers, whereas his son heard the opinion from him, an *individual*, "Therefore," he concluded, "it is your duty to leave the minority opinion in favor of the majority's."[41]

Despite the attempt to universalize the majority decisions, there remained, for a while, local deviations among dissenting rabbis, and these were even condoned. Thus, the Baraita states: "The law is in accordance with Beit Hillel, but he who wishes to follow Beit Shammai may," except that within a single dispute he must not follow the alleviations granted by both schools.[42] In the locality of Rabbi Eliezer, when a circumcision occurred on the Sabbath, all the accessory tasks, such as cutting trees for coal and forging the circumcision knife, were permitted on the Sabbath, in accordance with Rabbi Eliezer's opinion.[43] The Gemara implies that it is remarkable to permit these acts which could have been performed before the Sabbath, because logic and the general spirit of the Sabbath were on the side of Rabbi Akiva who declared that whatever could have been done before the Sabbath does not supersede the Sabbath, even in a situation where some desecration of the Sabbath is allowed.[44]

The rabbis tolerated local differences, even in basic areas of Sabbath observance, not only because "the words of both were the words of God," that is, the differing schools of thought were motivated by a common desire to sanctify life, but chiefly, because it took some time before the majority decision was universally disseminated and accepted.[45]

Even after universal standards were set in basic observance, local differences continued in areas of non-basic observance. Thus, the Mishna rules that one must not keep a dish hot by means of a stove heated with peat or wood unless the coal was removed or it was covered with ashes. According to Beit Shammai only water can be kept warm; and it may only be removed from the stove, but it may not be put back; but according to Beit Hillel even food may be kept warm, and it may be put back on the fire. Rabbi Yohanan interpreted the Beit Hillel decision to apply even where additional heating would be good for the dish; but according to the interpretation by Rav and Shmuel that would not be permitted even by Beit Hillel. The Gemara records this interesting statement made by Rabbi Ukva to Rabbi Ashi, "You who live near Rav and Shmuel follow their opinion; and we shall follow Rabbi Yohanan."[46]

In time the major rabbinic differences melted away because the rabbis were profoundly united on the fundamental principles: the vital role of the oral law and the binding power of the opinion of the majority rabbis. Minor differences were tolerated only until the majority decision could be disseminated and assimilated. This tolerance, however, was not extended to the Sadducees, for their approach threatened the entire structure of Torah and living as accepted by the Pharisees. Saducee differences, therefore, were fought with great force, even where they were not as extreme as some Pharisee disagreements, as the following quotation from the Tosephta will illustrate:

> The *lulav* supersedes the Sabbath on the first day of Succot, and the willow on the seventh. Once, when the seventh day occurred on a Sabbath, the people brought their willows on the eve of the Sabbath and placed them in the Temple court. The Sadducees (who say that since the willow on Succot is not specifically commanded in the Torah it does not supersede the Sabbath) took the willows and concealed them under the stones (which may not be handled on the Sabbath). On the Sabbath, the people discovered the willows, and pulled them out from under the stones. The *Kohanim* took the willows, and stood them up on the sides of the altar, for the Sadducees do not concede that the beating of the willows supersedes the Sabbath.[47]

In the quoted Tosephta we find strong resistance to the Sadducee attempt to prevent the beating of the willow on the Sabbath. Nevertheless, we are told that Rabbi Shimeon ordered the calendar calculators to arrange the calendar in a manner that would not necessitate taking of the willow on the Sabbath, because it has no Torah basis.[48]

The Torah commands that public sacrifices, involving numerous acts which are forbidden on the Sabbath, be offered on the Sabbath. The exemption of public worship and community needs from Sabbath restrictions seems to date back to the very beginning of the Sabbath institution,[49] and it was in effect until after the destruction of the Second Temple. Thus, witnesses were required to come and testify that they had seen the new moon even if they had to dese-crate the Sabbath to do so. The Baraita declares that when the Temple was in existence witnesses were allowed to dese-crate the Sabbath in order to testify concerning *all* new moons, because of the sacrifices brought on the new moon. However, when the Temple was destroyed Rabbi Yohanan decreed that desecration be permitted only for the new moons of Nisan and Tishre.[50] During the days of the Temple *lulavim* were taken in the synagogues on Sabbath, when it occurred on the first day of Succot. The *shofar* was sounded on Rosh Hashanah Sabbath in Jerusalem and its suburbs. When the Temple was destroyed, Rabbi Yohanan ruled that the *shofar* be sounded on Sabbath Rosh Hashanah only in cities with religious courts.[51]

3. From Sunset or Sunrise?

The traditional view is that the Sabbath has always begun at sunset on Friday. Some scholars, however, believe that at one time the Sabbath was observed from sunrise Satur-day, to sunrise Sunday. During the twelfth century, the Bible commentator, Abraham Ibn Ezra denounced and refuted this view.[52] Rabbinic exegesis and law generally sup-port Ibn Ezra's view. Thus, according to the Mishna, the day referred to in the law prohibiting the slaughter of an animal and its offspring in the same day, is reckoned from evening to evening, "as in creation," although (the Baraita adds) the day mentioned in the law requiring certain sacri-fices to be eaten on the day that they are offered, is reckoned from morning to morning.[53] The day cited in the law per-mitting nullification of a vow by a father or husband on the day the vow is made, also runs from evening to evening. Even if a vow is made by a woman on the Sabbath, the husband can nullify it only until dark.[54] All the Sabbath laws concerning the preparation of hot dishes for the Sabbath, candle lighting, and other preparations for the Sabbath are, obviously, based on the principle that the Sabbath begins at sunset.

In modern times Dr. Jacob Z. Lauterbach and others have revived the theory that the Sabbath once began at dawn of the seventh day. Dr. Lauterbach asserts that the statement in Matthew (28:1), "At the end of the Sabbath, as it began to dawn towards the first day of the week," preserved the older system which reckoned the Sabbath day from dawn to dawn. Dr. Lauterbach himself cites biblical and talmudic sources that are contrary to his theory; and he also mentions the Roman writers who refer to Friday evening candles, and the Samaritans who reckon the Sabbath in the traditional way. But he dismisses the last point by suggesting that the Samaritans may have broken with the Jews after the introduction of the traditional Sabbath day (during the Maccabean period) or that the Samaritans independently decided, on the basis of Leviticus 23:32, that the Sabbath began at sunset.[55]

According to Solomon Zeitlin, the biblical day was solar, and therefore, commenced at sunrise.[56] After the exiles returned from Babylonia (536 BCE), the lunar-solar calendar was introduced, and from then on the Sabbath was observed from sunset.[57] Another view is presented by Professor Cassuto. It is generally known that nomads begin the day at evening, and the wandering Israelites probably did likewise. After the conquest of Canaan, however, Professor Cassuto states, the day was generally reckoned as beginning at dawn, except the holy days which began at sunset, as the Torah specifies in connection with Passover and Yom Kippur. The Torah did not have to specify that the Sabbath and the other holidays also began at sunset, for agricultural work did not take place at night, anyway. Sacrifices followed the sunrise to sunrise routine of agriculturalists, but the holy days were observed in accordance with the pattern followed when the Israelites were nomads.[58]

We are inclined to the view that the Sabbath always began at sunset. Dr. Cassuto cites as proof that the biblical day began at dawn the Torah's commands (Exod. 12:18) to eat *matza* on the fourteenth, in the evening (what is today the evening of the fifteenth) and to begin the fast of Yom Kippur "on the ninth of the month in the evening" (Lev. 23:32), thus implying that the evening *follows* the day. This proof is invalid, for upon analysis we find that the Torah does not say "on the evening *of* the fourteenth," but rather "on the fourteenth of the month, in the evening. . .," which really means that the ban on leaven begins before the end of the fourteenth. Likewise, the Torah does not command that the fast be observed during the night of the ninth and the day of the tenth, but rather "on the ninth of the month, in the evening . . .", which simply means that the fast should be started while it is still the day of the ninth, before the evening of the tenth. Moreover, the Torah states, "But on the *tenth* of the seventh month . . ." (Lev. 23-27); but according to those who maintain that the biblical day began at dawn, half of the fast was really on the ninth, and the command should then have read, "But on the *ninth* of the seventh month"—which it does not.

Dr. Lauterbach quotes from Matthew to "prove" his contention that in the older system the Sabbath began at sunrise. Surely in Matthew's day the Sabbath began at sunset, even according to Dr. Lauterbach: Matthew, therefore, preserved not an older system but his own. How careful he was with Jewish tradition is apparent from his distortion of the Leviticus command ". . . to love thy neighbor as thyself" to mean "and you shall hate your enemy." (Matthew 5:43)[59]

Dr. Zeitlin cites instances in the Bible where it is written "day and night" (the word 'day' preceding the word 'night') as evidence that in Restoration days the day began at sunrise. This verbal sequence is very tenuous proof, for when people converse, they think of the day as commencing at sunrise. The Jews of eastern Europe surely began their Sabbaths and holidays at sunset, and yet in conversing they said, habitually, "tag und nacht." When working, one feels that the day begins upon waking in the morning, and that it continues through the period of work and wakefulness. Therefore, the sacrifices followed a sunrise to sunset routine. However, one prepares for an event *after* he awakens; therefore, the holy days began at sunset. Other laws, such as those concerning vows made by daughters and wives, and the prohibition of slaughtering an animal and its offspring in the same day, followed the traditional (sunset to sunset) routine.

Proof that the biblical day began at sunset can be found in the *manna* narrative which the Torah deliberately uses to emphasize the importance of the Sabbath. In the sixteenth chapter of Exodus, dealing with the discovery of *manna*, the Torah tells us that in response to the Israelite complaint, Moses promised that God would provide meat in the evening, and then bread in the morning. This sequence, repeated four times, is especially significant, for it involves observance.[60] In Judges (14:18) we learn that the people of the city told Samson "on the seventh day, before the setting of the sun . . .", implying that the seventh day, when the riddle could still be solved without penalty, ended *before* the setting of the sun.[61] In Nehemiah (13:19) it is stated, "And as the shadows began to fall on the gates of Jerusalem before the Sabbath . . .", implying the commencement of the Sabbath at sunset. In Esther (4:16), the request to fast three days is clarified with the words "night and day." This is significant, for in a ritual matter like a fast, the time sequence would be stated very carefully.[62]

The evidence tends to show that the biblical Sabbath started at sunset. If there ever was a time when the Sabbath day was reckoned from sunrise to sunrise, it certainly was not since the days of Ezekiel, when observance of the Sabbath as a holy institution became firmly established in Babylonia, for after the Sabbath was firmly established, it would have become impossible to transform a week night (Friday night, according to Lauterbach, etc.) into the beginning of the Sabbath; and it would have been regarded a desecration to turn Saturday night into a week night. This, added to other proofs cited, leads us to the conclusion that the biblical Sabbath began at sunset of the sixth day, although some of the major observances connected with the Sabbath were the result of evolutionary processes, and arose with the conditions rendering them either possible or desirable.

CHAPTER III

The Philosophy of the Sabbath

THERE ARE three basic reasons for the Sabbath, and they are stated directly or indirectly in five major references in the Torah. Genesis 1, and Exodus 20 describe the Sabbath as the *culmination of creation.* According to Deuteronomy 5, the purpose of the Sabbath is to *provide rest for servants, too.* Exodus 31 emphasizes the Sabbath as a sign of *God's covenant with, and His santification of, the Children of Israel.* Deuteronomy 5 (and probably also Exodus 20) *links the Sabbath with the Exodus.* This is not a fourth reason, but is auxiliary to the others.

The Torah implies, and rabbinic literature explicitly states, that creative work is divine, that a fixed weekly[1] day of rest is indispensable to life and creativity, and that this day of rest, linked to life, the direct concern of the Creator, is therefore blessed and sanctified. Hence, the Sabbath is for man's benefit, but it belongs to God. Man should rest and enjoy himself on the day, but he should also come closer to God through prayer, study and maintaining an atmosphere of joyous holiness. Briefly, we shall try to show how the Torah and the rabbis convey the reasons for the Sabbath.

The Torah tells us that God spent six days creating the world and man. "On the seventh day God completed His work which He had made. . . . And God blessed the seventh day, and sanctified it, because on it He rested from all His work, which God created to do."

That he who works is in holy partnership with God is

28

taught by Shemaya, as follows: "A man should love work, for as the Torah was given in a covenant, so was work, as it says, 'Six days work shall be done, and on the seventh day a solemn rest, holy to God . . . an eternal covenant between Me and the Children of Israel . . . for in six days the Lord made the heavens and earth'. . . ."[2]

The creative need for rest is pointed out in the following Midrash: "'And He rested. . . .' Can we speak of God as tiring and resting? This is only to teach us that if God, for Whom there is no fatigue and need of rest, rested, human beings who toil and tire should certainly rest."[3]

The Sabbath, like all of Judaism, is for the benefit of man.[4] However, its universal need, and its fixed nature, makes it subject to a law transcending that of man. This idea found expression in the Sabbath prayers, and was enunciated by Rabbi Yehudah Hanassi, who declared: "One concludes (the *Kiddush* and the prayer in the *Amidah* on a festival occurring on a Sabbath) with the words . . . 'Who sanctifies the Sabbath, Israel and the festivals,' for the Sabbath is eternally holy" (and its date need not be set by the *Beit Din*).[5] The principle was laid down in the *Mekhilta*: "And on the seventh day is a Sabbath of solemn rest to God . . ." (Exod. 31) teaches us that the Sabbath belongs to God and not to the *Beit Din*.[6]

The connection between the liberation from Egypt and the creation is pointed out by the following Midrash: God told Moses, "Urge the Israelites to remember all the miracles which I performed for you in Egypt, and the day that you went out from there, as I . . . commanded them to remember the day of the Sabbath, as a reminder of creation."[7]

A day of personal rest, for the preservation, enhancement and sanctification of life, is one aspect of the Sabbath. Related to it is making it possible for those under one's care, including servants and animals, to enjoy such rest. Consideration for God's creatures pervades biblical teachings. The Torah frequently relates consideration for the underprivileged to the Israelite experience in Egypt, as in the following, "Love the stranger, for you were strangers in the Land of Egypt" (Deut. 10:19). Hence, the Torah links rest for servants on the Sabbath with the Egyptian experience.

The Sabbath as a day of rest is based on a cosmic foundation, the universal need for regular rest. But the Sabbath, in its particular mode of observance, distinguishes the Jewish people as a holy nation and as a kingdom of priests. Israel was enslaved in Egypt and redeemed, in order to become a self-disciplined people that constantly strives to attain the highest levels of living and service. On the Sabbath the Jewish people reconfirm their covenant with God to be a holy people. On the Sabbath they recall that God created the world, that He guides history and that it was He who redeemed them from Egypt. They exemplify their covenant by preserving their life and enhancing it through physical rest, regulated, tension-releasing, joyous living, and by seeking spiritual upliftment through worship and study.

The Sabbath as a reminder of God and of Israel's sanctification is stressed by the prophet Ezekiel, especially in chapter 20: "And I brought them out of the Land of Egypt, and brought them to the desert. . . . I also gave them My Sabbaths, to be a sign between Me and them, to know that I am the Lord your God."

The Sabbath as a reminder of God the Creator and of Israel as God's witnesses is emphasized by the rabbis (*Mekhilta*):

> On one tablet it says, "Remember the Sabbath day to keep it holy" and facing it on the other it says, "Thou shalt not bear false witness." The Torah teaches us that whoever desecrates the Sabbath is as if he testified before

God that He did not create the world in six days and did not rest on the seventh day. But whoever rests on the Sabbath testifies before Him that He created the world in six and rested on the seventh.[8]

. . . The Sabbath adds holiness to Israel. "Why is this one's store closed? Because he keeps the Sabbath. Why does he not work? Because he keeps the Sabbath." Thus, he testifies that He who commanded and the world became, created it in six days and rested on the seventh; and thus it says, "And you are My witnesses, saith the Lord, and I am God" (Isaiah 43:12).[9]

Rest from work is, of course, of the essence of the Sabbath (which means 'cessation'—from work). This rest necessarily comes at the conclusion of a period of work. As we have seen, the Torah itself, by stating that God completed work on the seventh day, implies that the Sabbath was not a break from the preceding creation, but rather its culmination.

A reason for the abstention from all work, and for the rest of even one's animals (and even utensils, according to the Beit Shammai) can be inferred from Ibn Ezra's commentary on the verse, "In the seventh year there shall be a complete rest to the land, a sabbath to God." (Lev. 25:4) He writes, "It is a year of rest for the land, for during this year the land is not under your jurisdiction" (as the Torah declares in the chapter dealing with the sabbatical laws, ". . . for the earth belongs to Me; for you are temporary dwellers and tenants with Me"). This suggests that the weekly Sabbath, like the septennial sabbath, is a time when we realize that the world belongs to God. This feeling is induced by our cessation from all dispensable physical activity, for activity gives us a sense of possession and pre-occupation with self. Of course, the prohibition of the various activities sets the day apart, and gives it an atmosphere of distinctiveness and holiness; and it frees the observer from the routines and tensions of the week for wholesome enjoyment and spiritual uplift.

Elsewhere we wrote:

> Our religious precepts . . . are logical and psychological. Thus, Judaism requires that its holy days be observed from sundown to sundown. A holiday which is observed from sundown to sundown enables the observer to welcome it, and usher it out, by means of appropriate rituals. The day is complete and distinctive. The religious experience of welcoming, and taking leave from, the holiday makes the life of the observer also distinctive. Sometimes Judaism utilizes not a ceremony but an idea to achieve the necessary effect. Thus, the Sabbath is observed on the seventh day of the week to show that spiritual sublimation must follow physical creativity.[10]

The need to welcome the Sabbath, and to be aware of its commencement at sundown (contrary to the sectarians who sought to begin the Sabbath at sunrise) was stressed by the rabbis. Thus, Rabbi Hanina used to robe himself on Sabbath eve, and say, "Come, let us go to meet Sabbath the queen." Rabbi Yannai used to put on his cloak and say, "Welcome, O bride, welcome, O bride."[11] Rabbi Hamnuna said, "Whoever recites (on Sabbath eve) *Vayekhulu* (Gen., 2:1-3) is as if he became a partner of God in creation" (for he testifies that the Sabbath begins when God began it). Mar Ukva says, "If one recites *Vayekhulu*, the two angels who accompany him home (from the synagogue), place their hands on his head, and say, 'May your sins be removed.'" (Isaiah 6:7)

CHAPTER IV

Work Forbidden by the Torah

THE TORAH bans work on the Sabbath, but only in a few instances does it define or imply what constitutes such work. The Torah, however, states, "Do not do *any* work" (Exod. 20:10; Lev. 23:3; Deut. 5:14). In its prohibition of work on the festivals, the Torah states, "all work of labor do not do" (Lev. ch. 23). In its discussion of Passover, the first of the festivals, the Torah specifies, "only that which is eaten by all persons, that alone may be prepared for you" (Exod. 12:16). The implication is clear (as pointed out by Ibn Ezra, in his commentary on the above verse) that on the Sabbath even food preparation is forbidden. This is strengthened by the kinds of work the Torah does ban specifically. Thus, the making of a fire was forbidden (Exod. 35:3) even in food preparation (as pointed out by Ibn Ezra and Nahmanides). The Torah also specifies, "In plowing and reaping you shall rest" (Exod. 34:21), which is interpreted by Nahmanides to mean that even in matters involving the farmer's livelihood rest is mandatory. Carrying something from domain to domain is probably forbidden directly in Exod. 16:29; and according to one rabbinic view, the wood gatherer (Numbers 15:32-36) was punished because he carried four cubits in the public domain.[1] This category of work was singled out not only because of its social significance (as pointed out earlier), but, probably, also because it is usually involved in the process of food preparation.

During the days of the First Commonwealth the categories of work forbidden on the Sabbath were known to the people through regular observance. These, however, were forgotten after the destruction of the First Temple because of the prevailing neglect of the Sabbath. Ezra and the Soferim not only revived remembrance of the kinds of work prohibited, but they also proceeded to classify them. In due time, the classes of work became widely known and accepted. Consequently, we find that the Mishna, with apparent universal agreement by the rabbis, lists thirty-nine main ('avot' or parent) classes of work.[2] The later rabbis already did not know, and tried to ascertain, how these thirty-nine categories came to be regarded as parent classes. For the answer they went to what they considered the earliest definition (by implication) by the Torah of the idea of work. The construction of the Tabernacle in the desert involved various tasks which the Torah designates as work (Exod. 35:21, etc.). The rabbis, therefore, concluded that the traditional thirty-nine categories of work were the kinds of work involved in the construction of the Tabernacle.[3]

The thirty-nine categories of work are: 1) plowing, 2) sowing, 3) reaping, 4) binding sheaves, 5) threshing, 6) winnowing, 7) sorting (good fruit from bad), 8) grinding, 9) sifting (with a sieve), 10) kneading, 11) baking, 12) shearing wool, 13) washing wool, 14) beating wool, 15) dyeing wool, 16) spinning, 17) weaving, 18) making two loops, 19) weaving two threads, 20) separating two threads, 21) tying a permanent knot, 22) loosening a knot, 23) sewing two stitches, 24) tearing to sew two stitches, 25) hunting, 26) slaughtering, 27) flaying, 28) salting, 29) curing a skin, 30) scraping, 31) cutting, 32) writing two alphabet letters, 33) erasing in order to write two letters, 34) building, 35) pulling down a structure, 36) putting out a fire, 37) lighting a fire, 38) striking with a hammer, and 39) moving something from domain to domain.[4]

Moving an object from domain to domain, or moving it

four cubits within the public domain, is discussed at great length in the Talmud because of its universal application to persons and places and because of its social significance. Everyone, everywhere, at one time or another, faces the matter of moving either small or big objects. And the prophets were concerned with keeping masters from compelling their servants or porters to carry burdens on the Sabbath. Carrying from domain to domain was, probably, one of the first kinds of work banned. The verse, "Let no one go out of his place" (Exod. 16:29) may mean, as Tosafot interprets it, let no one go out from his place with his container to gather *manna.* This may also be why the first category of work discussed by the Mishna in *SHABBAT* is carrying an object from domain to domain.[5] Since many of the rules concerning Sabbath work are dealt with in relationship to this category of work, we shall also use it as our main example in discussing the various principles involved.

Moving an Object (*Hotza'ah*)

The Talmud speaks of four kinds of domain, only two of which figure in the Torah's ban on carrying. The latter two are: a private domain (*r'shut hayahid*) and a public domain (*r'shut harabim*). The private domain is an area at least four *tephahim* or handbreadths (each being about eight cm. according to Hanokh Albeck) by four by ten (either in height or depth), and it can be miles wide. A public domain[6] is a road, place or open alley way sixteen cubits (*amot*) wide and used by the public. The two other domains are: an enclosure 4x4x10 *tephahim,* but higher than 3; and seas, valleys, etc. The latter is called *carmelit,* traced by Rashi to *carmilo* (Isaiah 10:18), meaning gardenland. An exempt place (*makom patur*) is a place within the public domain less than 4x4 *tephahim,* but higher than 3; also the air in a public domain higher than ten, or a mound higher than, or a hole deeper than, three, but less than four *tephahim* wide. The Torah's ban applies to moving an object from private domain to public, or moving the object four cubits within the public domain,[7] and only if *one* person executes the entire act. That is, he has to pick up or move the object from its resting place, and he must put it down or bring it to rest.[8] Two who perform a task that one could have performed do not transgress according to the law of the Torah. Consequently, a man standing inside his house while handing something to a poor man on the outside, breaks a Torah law only if he puts the given object into the hand of the recipient.[9]

Motivation is essential in the concept of Sabbath work. One commits a transgression if he carries something from domain to domain only if that something has value at least to him. Thus, one transgresses if he carries out enough straw for a cow's mouthful; as much human food as a dry fig's bulk;[10] wine enough to mix a drink; milk enough for a gulp; oil to anoint the toe of a day old baby; water sufficient to rub off eye salve; enough rope to make a handle for a basket; blank paper of a size to write a tax collector's receipt; enough used paper to cover the mouth of a small perfume bottle; sufficient wood to cook the smallest egg; any amount of pepper; or any quantity of worn out sacred books, since they must be hidden away.[11]

The importance of *intent and purpose* is evident from the following: One transgresses if he carries out a piece of paper big enough for a tax collector's receipt; but if he carries out parchment (more valuable than paper) he transgresses only if it is enough at least for inscribing the *Sh'ma*.[12] One does not transgress if he carries out a vessel containing food less than the stated quantity, since the vessel is only an auxiliary to the food. One who carries out a living person in a bed does not transgress since the bed is only secondary to the person, and "the living person carries himself."[13] One transgresses if he carries out a living locust of any size since people keep it as a toy for children.[14]

An act, to be regarded work, must be performed in a normal manner. Thus, one does not transgress if he carries out an object with the back of his hand, or with his foot, or in his mouth, or in his shoe. However, he transgresses if he carries something out with his left hand, or inside his cloak, or on his shoulder (for the Levites in the Tabernacle carried in the latter manner).[15]

The care with which work is performed is another factor in the definition of Sabbath work. Thus, one does not transgress if he intended to keep something in front of him while carrying it out, but it slipped in back of him.[16] However, if he intended to keep it in back of him and it slipped to the front, he transgresses, for the care was better than he had intended. A woman carrying something in her apron transgresses either way, because her apron is likely to turn around and, therefore, the woman knew it might slip around.[17]

The ban on carrying from domain to domain does not apply to garments and ornaments, properly worn.[18] One may wear any garment of any material, but he may not cover himself with a box or rug, even to protect himself from rain, because these are not garments. One may not wear a sword, bow, spear, stick or shield, for their necessary use is shameful; but according to Rabbi Eliezer they are ornaments.[19]

It is forbidden to move an object from domain to domain whether one carries or throws it. According to Rabbi Akiva it is forbidden to throw something even from one private domain to another, if they are separated by a public domain.[20]

One commits a transgression when he removes an object from on top of a menorah which is ten *tephahim* high and four *tephahim* wide (making it a private domain), as does he who loads or unloads a wagon with the same measurements. One transgresses if he throws an object at a wall higher than ten *tephahim* high, and the object lodges in a hole four *tephahim* wide. A ball player transgresses if, while standing in a public place, he hits a ball to the wall from which it bounces back outside of four *amot*.[21]

A private domain need not be of lasting duration. Sometimes, it can be formed by rows of human beings, as the following two incidents illustrate. Once Rava's assistant brought in his master's bottles from the street while Rava was returning from lecturing at the *Beit Hamidrash*, because the rows of the people following Rava, appearing like walls, constituted a private domain. On the following Sabbath the servant wanted to bring in the bottles again, but Rava forbade it, for it is forbidden to circumvent the laws of the Sabbath deliberately.[22] Once the keys of the synagogue were forgotten. Rabbi Yirmiyahu advised that the keys be brought between the rows of people.[23]

As with all Sabbath work, making and putting out a fire must be *intended, for a constructive need.* Thus, one who puts out a lamp because of fear or for the sake of a sick person does not transgress the Torah; but he does, if he extinguishes the lamp in order to save oil or the wick.[24]

One who adds oil to a lamp transgresses, for it is like making a fire. However, if two lamps were present, one lit and one unlit, and a person intended to put out the lit one and instead he lighted the unlit one; or if he intended to light the unlit one but instead extinguished the lit one; in either case he does not transgress according to the Torah, for his intention was not realized.[25]

The Torah forbids a parent to give work to his minor son; but the parent need not stop his child from plucking grass on the Sabbath. However, if the minor wants to extinguish a fire, the parent is required to stop him, for the parent would be the beneficiary of such an act.[26]

According to the rabbinic interpretation of the Torah, one can commit a number of transgressions while working on the Sabbath, as for example when cooking or baking. In the days of the Temple (as we shall see later), one brought a sacrifice for every category of work he thus transgressed, unwittingly.[27]

According to the School of Ishmael, the Torah's prohibition of work on the Sabbath applies only to labor (*m'lekhet avodah*) but not to skills; therefore, the removal of bread from the oven (after it is baked) and the sounding of the *shofar*, being skills, are not forbidden by the Torah.[28]

One who forgetfully cooked on the Sabbath may eat the food, according to Rabbi Meir. Rabbi Yehudah says he may eat it *after* the Sabbath. Rabbi Yohanan the Alexandrian says *no one* may eat it. Rabbi Ishmael laid down the following rule: If the possibility of a sin offering or *karet* (probably excommunication) is involved, no one may eat of it.[29]

We stated earlier that work is a transgression only if it has value. Therefore, one transgresses only if he cut a double 'seit' (the seit being the span between the index and middle fingers) of hair or skin from an animal or fowl; and only if he cuts two human hairs; but according to Rabbi Eliezer he transgresses if he cuts even one. However, the Sages agree that one transgresses if he removes a single white hair from his black hair, for one does not wish to appear old, and removing a single white hair is therefore an important act falling within the category of *shearing*.[30]

One who tears in order to sew on two stitches transgresses, but he who tears in anger, or in mourning, and all who destroy are not transgressors, by Torah law. Rabbi Yehudah considers those who destroy in anger or in mourning, but not those who impair (*mekalkel*) generally, transgressors, for they give outlet to their emotions and each is, therefore, a "mender" (*metaken*).[31]

According to the rabbinic interpretation of the Torah, one is not a transgressor if he intends to pick up a detached fruit, and instead, unwittingly, plucks one from its plant, for this is not an act in error (*shogeg*) but an unintended one. A *shogeg* is one who *forgot* that the day is Sabbath or that the work is forbidden but he committed what he intended to do. According to the Torah, only intended work (*m'lekhet mahashevet*) is regarded as a Sabbath transgression.[32]

He who builds or hews stone or strikes a hammer or chisels or bores a hole on the Sabbath transgresses, if his work will last for a while, even though it is not permanent (like the Tabernacle constructed in the desert).[33] If one person puts down the stone and another the mortar, the second is regarded as the transgressor, for the structure cannot stand without mortar; but according to Rabbi Yehudah, both are transgressors.[34]

In the category of building are acts which, on the surface, may apear far removed from building. Thus, one who opens an abscess in order to leave it open and to peel it, commits a transgression within the category of building (or repairing) a door. But if he opens the abscess only to drain it, in which case he does not care that it closes again, he is no transgressor; and according to Shmuel it is even permissible by rabbinic law, for there is no repair, and where pain is involved the rabbis do not apply their restrictions.[35]

The same kind of work may be differently classified, depending on its purpose. Thus, he who removes a mound in his house transgresses as a builder; in the field, as a plower. He who fills a hole in his house commits an act of building; in the field, an act of plowing.[36] However, one may sweep his floor since he does not intend to sweep the dust into the holes. This is in accordance with Rabbi Shimeon's principle that the Torah's ban on Sabbath work does not apply to *work not needed per se* (*m'lakha she-einah tz'rikhah l'gufah*).[37]

It is Rabbi Eliezer's view that a woman who braids or combs her hair on the Sabbath, transgresses as a builder; and as a dyer, when she applies cosmetics; but the Sages regard such activities only transgressions of the spirit of the Sabbath (*sh'vut*).[38] One who pieces together a composite menorah transgresses as a builder. According to Rashi, he transgresses as one who wields a hammer, for building does not apply to vessels.[39]

In the days of Rabbi Yehudah ben Pazi there was a bed in the *beit hamidrash* which was covered with its curtain over an area of four *amot,* before the Sabbath, and completely, on the Sabbath. People thought that this was done with Rabbi Yehudah's knowledge; but upon investigation it was discovered that he had not been consulted, for according to the law, if most of the curtain is not spread over the bed before the Sabbath, there is the transgression of building when it is done on the Sabbath.[40]

One transgresses only if he completes a unit of work at one time. Thus, if he writes one letter of the alphabet in the morning, and another in the afternoon; or if he spins one thread in the morning and another in the afternoon, he is not regarded a transgressor (but according to Rabbi Gamliel he is).[41] However, one is a transgressor even if he completes only one unit of an entire operation, such as writing only the letters *Am* of the name Amiel. If one completes a name or a book by writing a ́needed single letter, he is a transgressor.[42]

As explained earlier, one is regarded a transgressor only if he alone completes the unit of work. Therefore, if two persons hold a pen and write neither transgresses. However, according to Rabbi Yehudah, the two are transgressors if one cannot do it alone.[43]

Again as explained earlier, the work must be somewhat enduring; ink and material which is written upon must be of lasting quality. Therefore, one who writes with fruit juice or in dust, etc. is not regarded a transgressor. The work has to be done normally; therefore, one who wrote with the back of his hand, or with his foot, or over what was already written, or on the ground or ceiling, or two letters on two pages not read consecutively does not transgress. An ambidextrous person writing with either hand transgresses.[44] One who writes one letter big enough for two small ones does not transgress; but he who erases a large letter in order to write two smaller ones does transgress.[45]

One who strikes any kind of blow with a hammer transgresses, for hammering was involved in the construction of the Tabernacle. To conclude a task is to commit a transgression within the category of hammering. Accordingly, Rav ruled that one who opens a shirt collar (or the pocket of a new suit) transgresses as one who wields a hammer, for he concludes work. Rav explains that this is different from opening a jug on the Sabbath, which is permitted for the sake of guests, for the collar is part of the garment, but the cap of the jug is only cemented on with mortar.[46]

One who plows, somewhat, or weeds, or trims a plant, or prunes it transgresses. One who plucks plants from the ground, to improve it, transgresses as a plower; if to improve the plants, he transgresses as a sower. One who forgetfully plants on the Sabbath need not uproot it; although he must uproot what he plants during the sabbatical year, because he will not deliberately transgress the laws of the Sabbath, whereas he might neglect the laws of the sabbatical year.[47]

Winnowing and sifting are similar types of work, and yet they are listed as different categories because, according to Abbaye and Rava, both types were involved in the construction of the Tabernacle, and therefore are important enough to list separately.[48] According to Rabbi Eliezer, making buttermilk comes within the category of sifting; milking, within the category of threshing, "for the milker removes food from hidden places," as explained by Rashi.[49] The squeezing of fruit for its juice belongs in the category of threshing.[50]

One transgresses if he makes or unties a camel driver's or sailor's knot (which are similar to those used in the construction of the Tabernacle). The knot must be well-made and durable; and according to Rabbi Meir, if the knot can be untied with one hand, one does not transgress.[51]

One transgresses if he traps a non-domesticated animal. One transgresses if he shuts in a gazelle which entered an enclosure; but two who do it are not transgressors (by Torah law), unless one cannot do by himself, in which case, according to some rabbis, both are transgressors.[52] If a deer enters an enclosure with two doors, and two persons close the doors, the second person is the transgressor. One who traps a lame, sick or old deer is not a transgressor, for the deer is as if already trapped. However, one transgresses if he captures a sleeping or blind deer, for it could have escaped. One does not transgress if he closes a door and later finds a deer in the enclosure, or if he puts on his cloak, and then finds a bird in it, for he did not plan to trap the animal.[53]

One who catches flies on the Sabbath transgresses, according to Rabbi Meir, but not according to Rabbi Yehudah, because people do not ordinarily hunt flies. One who captures locusts early in the morning, at the time of the dew, does not transgress, for they are blinded and easy to catch. According to the majority rabbinic opinion, one who captures locusts and other insects at any time is not a transgressor, for such are not customarily hunted.[54]

One who traps or wounds one of the eight crawling animals listed in the Torah (*Lev.* 2:29-30), animals that have skins and are ordinarily hunted, transgresses. Wounding is a derivative (*toldah*) of threshing or dyeing. According to Rav, slaughtering is also a derivative of dyeing, in addition to being a parent (*av*) or basic category of work, involved in the construction of the Tabernacle.[55] Rabbi Eliezer says he who kills a louse on the Sabbath is as if he killed a camel.[56]

All Sabbath food-quantities (the amounts regarded as valuable in carrying, reaping and grinding) must be equivalent to the bulk of a dry fig.[57]

One must not desecrate the Sabbath even in order to perform a *mitzvah,* for the Torah, by placing the laws concerning the Sabbath next to those concerning the construction of the Tabernacle implied that even the construction of the Tabernacle was not permitted on the Sabbath.[58] One must not, therefore, work on a scroll, phylacteries, mezuzah or ark curtain on the Sabbath, for these things can be done before or after the Sabbath.[59] Work is forbidden on all Sabbaths, including those during the sabbatical year.[60] The Torah, says the *Mekhilta*, purposely repeated the command to keep the Sabbath following the laws of the sabbatical year to teach that one must not reason that since the entire seventh year is called sabbath (and is a reminder of God), the weekly Sabbath need not be kept during it.[61]

CHAPTER V

Rabbinic Prohibitions

THERE ARE activities which would be permitted by the Torah, but the rabbis prohibited them for one of the following four reasons: 1) in order to prevent the transgression of a Torah law, this precautionary decree (*g'zeira*) being a hedge (*s'yag*) to the Torah; 2) if on the eve of the Sabbath something was not intended to be used during the Sabbath because the thing was connected with a forbidden activity, or it was in an unattractive state, or its use could lead to loss of money, then it may no longer be used during the Sabbath, and it is said to be *muktza* (set aside from use during the Sabbath); 3) an article that came into existence when the Sabbath had already begun, so that one was not prepared for its use on the eve of the Sabbath, is said to be *nolad* (born during the holy day), and may not be used during the Sabbath; 4) activities not in the general spirit of the Sabbath are forbidden because of *sh'vut* (to keep from dispensable, physical routines and to maintain a Sabbath atmosphere of complete rest).

1. Precautionary decrees or *g'zeirot*

According to the School of Rabbi Ishmael, the Torah permits the sounding of the *shofar* on the Sabbath and the removal of baked bread from the oven, because these are not tasks but skills. The rabbis, however, forbid the sounding of the *shofar* even on a Rosh Hashanah Sabbath lest, in seeking to learn to blow it, the blower will carry it to his teacher, on the Sabbath. To prevent a possible student from forgetfully carrying a *megillah* to his teacher, the *megillah* is not read on a Purim Sabbath.[1]

The following rabbinic restrictions were instituted in order to *prevent* the commission of acts forbidden by the Torah.

On Friday toward dark, a tailor must not go out of his house with his needle stuck in his garment, lest he will forget and carry it *after* dark; nor may a scribe leave his house with his pen stuck behind his ear, for the same reason.[2]

Apparel or jewelry which the wearer is likely to remove in order to show it to another, and then forgetfully carry four cubits in the public domain, may not be worn outside one's house. Thus, a woman may not go out wearing bands of wool or of flax if these are not sewn on the head dress; nor may she go out with a "golden city" (a crown shaped like Jerusalem) or with nose rings.[3] According to the sages, a woman may not go out with an ordinary false tooth lest it arouse ridicule, so that she will remove and carry it; nor with a gold one lest she remove it, to show off; but with a silver tooth, which will not arouse ridicule, and which, as Rashi explains, she is not apt to remove for ostentatious reasons, she may go out.[4] A woman may not go out with her perfume flask or spice box; and according to Rabbi Meir, if she does she breaks even a Torah law, but according to Rabbi Eliezer she *may*.[5] A woman bathing ritually on the Sabbath may not put on such articles of clothing as bands of wool or flax not sewn on to the head dress, which she might forgetfully remove and carry four cubits in the public domain.[6]

The prohibition of wearing apparel which one might remove and carry four cubits in the public domain applies to men as well as to women. Thus, a man may not go out wearing a single sandal lest he will remove it, when laughed at; nor may he go out with an amulet prepared by a non-expert or with phylacteries.[7]

One must not stand in one domain and drink water in another domain unless his head and most of his body are where he stands. However, a person may pour his dirty water from a window to a garbage heap below, if the heap is ten *tephahim* high. (The action is thus from one private domain to another.) One may not stand on the street and open a door in a private domain, lest he will move the key to where he stands. The sages, citing the example of a poultry market, where permission was given to hang the key on the window above the door, permit the opening of the door (but not the moving of the key).[8]

One may not move an object from a public or private domain to a *carmelit,* and vice versa, or from one ship to another.[9] Rav ruled that one may carry everywhere on a ship.[10]

According to the rabbis, the Torah ban on making a fire and heating by it, does not apply to sun and natural water heat. However, the use of such heat is forbidden by rabbinic law, where the user or spectator could be misled into believing that heating by fire derivatives is also permissible. Thus, one may not poach an egg in a sun-heated cloth lest one think that it is also permissible to cook an egg by placing it next to a heated kettle. (This means that the derivative—*toldah*—of sun heat is forbidden lest one come to permit also the *toldah* of fire.) One may not roast an egg in the heated sand or dust of the road, lest he will do it also in hot ashes, or lest he move the hard earth while sticking the egg into it (which is like plowing).[11] Rabban Shimeon ben Gamliel permits the cooking of an egg in boiling lime (for lime is a *toldah* of sun heat), but not in heated dust (lest he move it).[12]

Once the people of Tiberias led a duct of cold water through a hot spring. The rabbis said that such heated water is forbidden even for drinking.[13] The Talmud Yerushalmi, however, states that the use of sun heat and its derivatives are permissible; and the people of Tiberias, therefore, did not desecrate the Sabbath.[14]

Shmuel ruled that the Torah prohibition to extinguish a fire does not apply to red-hot iron, but the rabbis forbade such activity (lest one put out wood or coal also). However, where public danger is involved, the rabbis removed their restriction; therefore, it is permissible to cool a piece of red-hot iron lying on the street, where passers-by might be injured.[15]

One of the most interesting disputes between the Schools of Shammai and Hillel concerns self-completing work begun before the Sabbath. According to the Tosephta, Beit Shammai base their opinion on the verse, "Six days you shall labor, and do *all* your work" (Exod. 2:9), which they interpret to mean that all work must be completed *before* the seventh day. But Beit Hillel interpret the verse to mean that one may work the entire six days even if the work continues automatically into the seventh.[16] Underlying the Beit Hillel opinion is the idea that work is judged by its start, or by the release of its energy and setting it on its way. This is implied in a law found in the Yerushalmi, which is stated as follows.

Said Rabbi Eleazer: "One may declare on the Sabbath eve, 'May this grain become *trumah* (heave-offering) tomorrow,' for, although it does not become *trumah* until the Sabbath, the declarer is not regarded as a mender *(metaken)* on the Sabbath (as he would if he made his declaration on the Sabbath). But one may not say on the Sabbath, 'May this become *trumah* tomorrow,' for his declaration renders the grain ritually fit, although he cannot eat it until after the Sabbath."[17] That is, the mending (tikun) begins with the declaration, and it is then that the work is said to have been done, although the actual work is not completed until the declaration takes effect, when the grain becomes trumah.

It may be, however, that Beit Shammai, too, accept the idea that work is done when the energy propelling it to completion is released, for the Babylonian Talmud explains the various Shammaiitic restrictions in instances of self-completing work as g'zeirot, lest he will complete work. Following are several illustrations of the foregoing.

According to Beit Shammai ink and dye stuffs may not be cooked on Friday unless there is time for them to be wholly cooked before the Sabbath; but according to Beit Hillel it is permissible.[18] According to Beit Shammai bundles of flax may not be put into the oven on Friday, unless there is time for them to steam while it is yet day. Nor may wool be put into a cauldron unless there is time for the wool to absorb the color before sunset; but Beit Hillel permit these things. Beit Shammai say one may not set traps for animals or fish unless they can be caught before the Sabbath, but Beit Hillel permit it.[19]

Beit Shammai say one must not sell to a heathen or place a load on his back, or load his beast on Friday, unless the heathen will have time to reach a nearby place before dark. Beit Hillel say that the heathen's leaving the house is sufficient; however, he must leave, for otherwise people will think that the Jew sold to the heathen on the Sabbath. Beit Shammai say one must not give hides to a heathen tanner or clothes to a heathen launderer unless the work can be completed before the Sabbath. Beit Hillel permit it.

Both Schools agree that one may not roast meat, onions and eggs on Friday unless the dish can be edibly roasted while it is yet day, lest he will try to hasten the roasting by removing the ashes from the coal, during the Sabbath. However, the Passover sacrifice may be lowered into the oven toward dark for the members of the group participating in the celebration will keep one another from forgetfully removing the ashes.[20]

Beit Shammai and Beit Hillel agree that it is permissible to lay down olive press beams or the wine press rollers while it is yet day, for the release of the liquid already took place while it was still day, and during the Sabbath the liquid oozes by itself.[21]

Bread may not be put into the oven toward evening on Friday, unless there is time for the bottom surface to encrust.[22] One must not place wheat in a water mill unless it can be ground before dark, lest the noise cause people to say that he grinds on the Sabbath.[23]

During the Sabbath, one may not read, even in holy scriptures, by the light of a lamp, lest he will tilt the lamp, to give it more oil (which is a transgression by Torah law). Rabbi Ishmael told that he once thought that he would remember not to tilt the lamp, but he almost did, and then he learned to appreciate the validity of the rabbinic precaution. According to Rabban Shimeon ben Gamliel *pupils* may read by light of the lamp, for they are in awe of their teacher, and will be afraid to tilt the lamp. According to the Talmud Yerushalmi, pupils will not tilt the lamp, because they would prefer to let it go out, so that they should not have to study. One may examine a bowl of food by the light of the lamp to make sure that *it is safe to eat.*[24]

One may not look into a metal mirror lest he will use it to remove a white hair.[25] *One* person who has bathed in the waters of a cave or of the hot springs of Tiberias may not carry the towel (or towels) that he has dried himself with, lest he will wring it; but more than one, using even one towel (although soaking) may carry it, for each will remind the other if one should forgetfully want to wring the towel.[26]

One may not climb a tree lest he will break off a twig; nor may one ride on an animal lest he will cut off a branch to strike the animal; nor may one swim, lest he will make himself a swimmer's balloon; nor may one clap his hands, musically, or dance, lest he will come to repair a musical instrument. The Talmud Yerushalmi, quoted by Rabbi Hananel explains that one must not climb a tree lest he will shake off its fruit; he must not ride on an animal, because he is commanded to give it rest; and he must not clap his hands in anger. According to Rabbi Eleazer, all forms of noisemaking are forbidden on the Sabbath.[27]

One may not handle a composite menorah (even a new one), lest it fall apart, and he will put it together (and this would be a transgression in the category of building). Old shoes and sandals may not be scraped lest he peel off the leather, but they may be wiped; however, they may not be oiled, for this is a form of curing skin. Rabban Shimeon ben Gamliel says shoes and sandals never worn before may not be put on on the Sabbath, for the wearer breaks them in, and this is a form of mending a vessel.[28]

Medicinal preparations for non-dangerous diseases are not permitted lest one will grind up the ingredients. For the benefit of the sick, Rabbi Meir permits things forbidden only by rabbinic law. However, Rabbi Meir, when he was sick, refused to let his students prepare for him a mixture of oil and wine. Asked, "Are you negating your own opinion?" he answered, "I never went contrary to the opinions of my colleagues" in practice.[29]

One whose garments become drenched may spread them

out in the sun privately but not publicly lest people suspect him of washing on the Sabbath. However, the accepted rule is that *what is forbidden publicly is also forbidden privately.*[30]

2. Muktza

Certain articles may not be used on the Sabbath because their would-be user did not intend to use them during the Sabbath, or because ordinarily they are utilized for work forbidden on the Sabbath. Such articles are said to be *muktza,* that is, by their ordinary use, or by their owner's intention, they are set apart from Sabbath use. *Muktza* is not forbidden by the Torah, but the rabbis found some basis for their prohibition in the verse, "And it shall be on the sixth day, and they shall prepare that which they will bring in" (Exod. 16:5). This is interpreted to mean that one should *prepare,* also in *intention,* whatever he will use on the Sabbath.[31] There are several kinds of *muktza,* as the following will illustrate.

1) A vessel may not be put under a lamp to collect the oil, unless it was placed there before the Sabbath. The reason is: The oil may not be handled, since it was set aside for a function forbidden on the Sabbath—kindling. Since the vessel becomes subordinate to the oil, when one places it to collect the oil, it, too, may not be handled. To put it there during the Sabbath means, therefore, that one is removing it from a state of permissibility to one of forbidden use.[32]

2) A lamp that was burning during Sabbath (and hence could not be handled then lest the holder extinguish it) may not be handled at all that Sabbath because it became *muktza* during the time it was burning.[33]

3) According to another rabbi, an earthenware lamp that

was already used may no longer be handled on Sabbath, because of its unclean or repulsive condition.[34]

4) All household utensils and their parts, the Mishna states, may be handled, even if they became detached on the Sabbath. One may even handle a hammer to crush nuts and a needle to remove a thorn. Rabbi Yose adds that all utensils may be handled except a large saw and the pin of a plow, for these are set aside for their particular work.[35] The Gemara explains that this is a case of *muktza* because of possible loss of money, that is, because the owner does not want to break the saw and the plow pin, he sets them aside completely and does not want them used on the Sabbath (and therefore, according to all the rabbis he may not use these implements).[36]

The following laws fall within the above four classes of *muktza*.

Beit Shammai say that one may not remove from the table bones and shells; to remove them, he lifts the board and shakes them off; but Beit Hillel permit the direct removal. According to both, however, it is permissible to remove even tiny crumbs for they can be fed to cattle.[37]

A man may carry his child (in a courtyard covered by an *eruv*), even if the child holds a stone (which may not be handled on the Sabbath). One may carry a basket with perishable fruit (which would be ruined by being thrown to the ground) even if there be a stone in it. If a stone is on top of a jar, one should tilt the jar so that the stone will fall off. A person who wants to use a pillow on which there is money may shake the pillow so that the money will fall off. This, however, may be done only if one forgot the money there on Sabbath eve; but if one left it there, knowingly, the pillow becomes the base for a forbidden article, and he may not shake off the money.[38]

According to Rav, a well person may eat of the food

cooked for a sick person, but not of an animal slaughtered
on the Sabbath for a sick person. The food could have been
eaten even before it was cooked, and so it was not *muktza*
for the well person; whereas the meat of the animal slaughtered on the Sabbath was not ready to be eaten by the well
person, that is, for him the animal was *muktza*.[39]

According to Rav, one may place pillows under an animal
that has fallen into a pond, so that the animal should be
able to help itself out, if the animal cannot be kept and fed
where it fell until after the Sabbath. This is permitted,
although by placing the pillows under the animal, one
removes them from permissible use on the Sabbath (having
become subordinate to something forbidden). The latter,
however, is forbidden only by rabbinic law which does not
apply where pain to living creatures is involved, for the prevention of such pain is commanded by the Torah.[40]

3. *Nolad*

Related to the concept of *muktza* is the one of *nolad*,
something which comes into existence after the Sabbath (or
festival) has started. Thus, the Mishna states that an egg
hatched during a festival by a hen (kept for its eggs) may
not be eaten then, according to Beit Shammai (in the
Gemara version) because it was not in existence prior to the
festival (or Sabbath). According to Beit Hillel, this form of
nolad is permissible on the Sabbath, for people do not regard
it lightly, and a justified alleviation will not lead to the
abuse of the Sabbath elsewhere. For this reason one may
cut up vegetables for the cattle during Sabbath.[41]

4. *Sh'vut*

The rabbis forbade on the Sabbath certain activities and
weekday routines in order to preserve a spirit of Sabbath

restfulness. The *Mekhilta* deduces this from the verse, "But My Sabbaths keep" (Exod. 31:13).[42] Thus, one may loosen bundles of hay before cattle, but he may not break unripe corn or carob stalks for them. One may not break up dry figs and carobs for old people, but he may break the fruit with the handle of a knife to vary it from the weekday routine. Water may be poured on bran served to cattle, but the bran and water must not be kneaded. Water may not be set before bees and doves, for these can find their own water, but it may be set before geese and fowl.[43]

One may not walk to the limit of a Sabbath-day's journey, in order to be there ready to work when the Sabbath is over. However, for the sake of performing a *mitzvah,* such as to arrange a wedding or burial, it is permissible.[44] One must not pay a Jew to guard his child or animal on the Sabbath. However, one may pay by the week or longer periods, including the Sabbath (and, therefore, the watchman is responsible in case of negligence). The guard, however, must not ask for a week's wages but only for a minimum of ten days (which would not make the Sabbath stand out). One may guard plants against birds, but he must not clap his hands or stamp his feet, as he does on a weekday.[45]

One may clear away as many as five bales of hay on the Sabbath, to make room for his guests and students, but he may not clear away a whole store.

Calves and donkeys may be pulled along on the highway; and a mother may pull her child along; but according to Rabbi Yehudah, she may do so only if her child can at least toddle.[46]

One may not write even one letter of the alphabet nor may he weave even one thread, etc. Although these acts are not units of Sabbath work, yet the Torah implies the desirability of *total rest* when it commands that the Sabbath be kept as *Shabbat Shabbaton.* Therefore, one may not climb

a tree or ride on an animal or swim or clap his hands musically, or dance or marry or be divorced, etc.[47] (Some of these
things are forbidden also lest one come to greater desecration, as explained earlier.)

One who forgot to remove his bread from the oven before
the Sabbath, may remove enough for three meals, and he
may invite others to do likewise; but he may not remove
the bread with a baker's shovel but only with a knife, in
order to make a distinction from the weekday routine.[48]

One may not board a ship for a business voyage on the
Mediterranean (that is, on a sea of considerable size) less
than three days before the Sabbath, but to perform a *mitzvah*
it is permissible to embark even on Friday. If the ship
anchors on the Sabbath, the voyager should disembark only
if the ship arrived before the Sabbath within the limits of
the Sabbath day's journey (the 2000 cubits allowed a person
from his dwelling or city), and only if the gangplank was
put down by heathens for heathen passengers. Once it happened that Rabban Gamliel and the elders arrived at their
destination after dark on Friday, and they disembarked, because according to Rabban Gamliel's reckoning they had
arrived within the *t'hum* (the 2000 cubits) before sundown,
and because the gangplank was put down for the use of the
other passengers.[49] In accordance with the principle of
sh'vut, the rabbis forbade a Jew to ask a heathen to perform
work for him on the Sabbath. Work done by a non-Jew for
a Jew, such as picking fruit, may not be enjoyed by the
Jew until after the Sabbath is over, by which time the Jew
could have done it himself.[50] However, where the non-Jew
does something for his own benefit, without thinking of its
likely use by the Jew, the latter may enjoy it even on the
Sabbath. The following will illustrate the above.

A Jew must not say to his non-Jewish partner, "Take
the Sabbath income as your share and I shall take as mine

a weekday's." However, if they formed their partnership on that basis it is permissible, for this means that the Jew never received profit for work done on the Sabbath.[51]

A Jew must not ask a non-Jew to light a lamp for him; but if the non-Jew lit it for himself, the Jew may use it. Likewise, a Jew may use the balance of the water a non-Jew drew for his own animal, from a public well. (Drawing water from a well is like carrying from one domain to another.) A Jew may use a gangplank put out by a non-Jew for his own use, after the non-Jew has descended from the boat, as was done by Rabbi Gamliel and the elders.[52]

A Jew may not use funeral flutes brought on the Sabbath by a non-Jew for a Jew. A casket or grave made on the Sabbath for a Jew may never be used for a Jew (as a penalty, according to Rashi's commentary); but if made for a non-Jew, the casket or grave is permissible for a Jew (after the Sabbath, of course).[53]

The rabbis permit things usually prohibited because of the principle of sh'vut, where a mitzvah has to be performed. Therefore, a Jew who buys a house in Eretz Israel from a heathen may ask a non-Jew to write the deed on the Sabbath.[54]

According to Beit Hillel, charity may be allocated to the poor on the Sabbath; marital matches may be arranged; and one may pray for the recovery of the sick on the Sabbath.[55]

A husband may annul his wife's vows on the Sabbath, since it has to be done on the same day. A ritual pool (mikveh) may be measured on the Sabbath.[56]

Some rabbis imposed upon themselves undeclared restrictions out of deference to the uneducated (and in some instances out of deference to minority rabbis whose localities they were visiting) who customarily kept these restrictions, or, lest these uneducated become lax in other areas of Sabbath observance. Thus, the Tosephta teaches, one may wear wide sandals on the Sabbath, and we do not say that the wearer might remove and carry them four cubits in a public domain. Once Yehudah and Hillel, sons of Rabban Gamliel, wore such sandals in Beiri, where the people regarded such practice forbidden. When the people deploringly commented, "We have never seen the like of it," the brothers removed their sandals, and gave them to their servants.

One may sit down on a heathen bench during the Sabbath, without fear that he might be suspected of having used the bench for selling. Once, on a Sabbath, Rabban Shimeon ben Gamliel sat down on such a bench in Acco, where the people do not do it, and the people remarked, "We have never seen the like of it." Rabban Shimeon thereupon sat on the ground, and he did not say, "It is permissible." The Gemara adds that the people overseas, not being visited often by rabbis, exaggerate alleviations and tend to become lax; therefore, the rabbis were extremely careful not to do anything which could lead to neglect of the Sabbath.[57]

The Torah commands that one's animals, too, rest on the Sabbath; therefore, one transgresses when he leads his beasts while they carry his burdens.[58] Rabbinic law also forbids placing on the animal any equipment that is not primarily for the comfort and protection of the animal but for the holding and safeguarding of the burdens. Equipment that might fall off, making it necessary for the owner to pick it up, and possibly causing him to carry it, forgetfully, four cubits in the public domain, is also forbidden. Accordingly, Rabbi Yehudah says that goats may not go into the public domain with their udders bound up, if the binding is not intended to keep the udders dry but to collect the milk, for since the cloth is not tied tightly, it might fall off, causing the owner to pick it up and carry it. A cow may not go out with the strap between her horns. Rabbi Eliezer ben Azariah's cow did go out with her strap between her horns, and the rabbis were displeased. Equipment not considered a burden, or that which is regarded as necessary for the protection or comfort of the animal, and hence permitted on the Sabbath, includes: curbs and chains, a donkey's saddle-cloth, if fastened on before the Sabbath; the strapping of a ram; bandages on a wound and casts on a fracture; and bells muted with soft rags.[59]

5. Rabbinic Alleviations

In the Talmud Yerushami we find this significant statement by Rabbi Yosah: "See how the sages alleviated the rigors of the Sabbath, that even vessels not ordinarily used on the Sabbath were permitted for the sake of the Sabbath!"[60] This seems to bear out George F. Moore, who wrote, "What is new in the rabbinical laws of the Sabbath is not the introduction of every kind of work—that is emphatically biblical—but the direct or round-about provision for the necessary exceptions. . . ."[61] Although we believe that Dr. Moore over-states his case, the rabbis sought to foster observance of the Torah laws and the spirit of the Sabbath by means of "'hedges" and limitation of weekday routine. Nevertheless, it is true that the rabbis shied from *unnecessary* restrictions. Sometimes they even dispensed with already established restrictions lest insistence on adherence impel a graver transgression. Thus, a man who finds himself on the road when Sabbath is about to begin may let his non-Jewish companion carry his purse for him. If no non-Jew is present, he may place his purse on his donkey. When he reaches the closest city, he removes the things he may handle, and the bag containing his purse he lets fall off. The Talmud explains that the traveller is allowed to give

the purse to his non-Jewish companion because otherwise
he might be tempted to carry it himself.[62] According to
Rabbi Yehudah ben Lakish, a man may save the deceased
body of his kin from a fire for otherwise, in his anguish, he
might be led to extinguish the fire.[63] The following are
instances of rabbinic alleviations for the reason of prevent-
ing a greater desecration or in order to render the Sabbath
more comfortable, or for healing purposes (not involving
the possibility of forgetfully grinding ingredients).

Small girls may go out with threads or chips in their
ears (preparatory to their wearing of earrings). A woman
may go out with her veil and with her cloak looped over
her shoulder. She may use a stone or coin for a *button* (provided these were put on before the Sabbath) because being
subordinate to the garment, they are not *muktza*.[64]

According to Rabbi Meir, a man may go out with a
locust's egg (regarded as a cure for earache) or a jackal's
tooth (a cure for sleepiness) or with a nail from the gal-
lows of one crucified, if used for healing purposes; but
according to the sages these things are forbidden even on
weekdays for they are in imitation of the heathens, who
place their trust in such things.[65]

Food may be kept warm by being covered with things
that will preserve but not increase its heat.[66] One may not
add cold water to a partially-filled heated container in order
to heat the new water; but one may add water in order to
make the already heated water lukewarm.[67]

One may eat or drink anything of curative nature, if
healthy people use it, too. A person who has a toothache
may not gargle with vinegar, but he may swallow it, although
thereby his toothache is cured. One whose loins ache may
not anoint them with wine and vinegar, but he may anoint
them with oil, for healthy persons, too, use oil; but he may
not anoint with rose-oil, for it is expensive, and it is

obviously for a cure, unless he is a nobleman who uses such oil ordinarily. Rabbi Shimeon says that all Israelites are noblemen (and may anoint their aching loins with rose-oil).[68]

One may not prepare pickling brine (in large quantity), but he may prepare salt water and use it with his bread or cooked food. Rabbi Yose forbids the preparation of even a small quantity for use with food, for he regards such preparation which preserves the food, like skin curing. However, it is permissible when one adds oil (for the oil keeps the water and salt from mixing too well).[69]

The following knots are permissible on the Sabbath: the tying of a woman's apron strings, her hair-net, the straps of shoes and sandals, the strings of bottles of oil or wine, and of a pot of soup. According to Rabbi Eliezer ben Yaakov, the stall of an animal may be roped off, to prevent its exit. One must not knot the rope of a well bucket that broke, but he may tie it loosely.[70]

Ice must not be broken up in order to liquefy it, for turning it into water is work; but one may break up the ice in a cup or dish, in order to chill wine.[71]

Before the Sabbath, one may put a salved bandage on a wound, and wear it during the Sabbath; but if it falls off, he may not replace it lest he will scrape the wound.

Spice sticks may be given to a sick person to crack or chip for smelling purposes.[72]

Rabbi Meir permits things forbidden by rabbinic law, for the benefit of the sick.[73]

It is permissible for a bridegroom to be with his bride, even if they are together for the first time, on the Sabbath.[74]

One may open or close a door behind which there is a lamp, although the draft puts out the lamp. However, Rav denounced such action.[75]

Beds may be made on the Sabbath for the same day but not for after Sabbath.[76]

One may break a jug to get out its needed food, provided he does not aim to make a vessel, such as an opening to pour; for if he does aim to do it, he is not an impairer (m'kalkel—which the Rabbis permitted in case of need, provided it is not a preliminary to a constructive act), but he does a constructive and therefore forbidden act.[77]

Nuts and pomegranates may be cracked for use on the same day. Dishes may be rinsed for use on the same day; therefore, the afternoon dishes may not be rinsed. However, glasses may be washed at all times and in any number for there is no set time for drinking. One may also make a number of beds.[78]

One may borrow from his neighbor jars of oil or wine or loaves of bread, provided he does not say, "Lend me for a while," lest the lender, in fear of forgetting, will write it down. If the lender does not trust the borrower, he may request a garment as surety. One may compute how many portions he needs for his guests but not from a written list lest he forgetfully erase.[79]

One may read official public announcements on the Sabbath.[80]

A cooked dish may be placed into a pit to keep it cool. One may place a jar of oil opposite a fire to remove the chill of the oil.[81]

One may wash his face, hands, and feet with water heated on Friday, but not his whole body, even part by part.[82]

One may bathe in the waters of Tiberias or in the Mediterranean, but not in the Dead Sea, for it looks as if he does it for a cure. However, for ritual bathing, where one dips and comes right out, it is permissible, except for a convert, for to him bathing is the completion of his conversion, and therefore it is like mending on the Sabbath.[83]

One may enter a public bath house for sweating but not for bathing. Rabbi Yehudah permits showering in cold but not in warm water, but according to Rabbi Shimeon it is permissible (and according to Rabbi Meir even in cold water it is forbidden).[84]

One may not run on the Sabbath for exercise (but to the house of study it is permissible); but one may walk even a whole day.[85]

One may walk on grass, for the law is in accordance with Rabbi Shimeon that unintended work is not a transgression.

One may anoint or rub his stomach but not massage it, for it looks like a weekday routine. One whose foot is sprained may not pour cold water on it, for it looks as if he does it for a cure, but he may wash it as usual, although thereby he is healed.[86]

Holy scriptures, written in Hebrew, may be saved from a fire by being brought into an adjacent courtyard, even when not covered by an *eruv*. Blessings and amulets may not be saved from fire, although they contain letters of God's name or passages from the Torah. Nor may sectarian books be saved, though they contain God's name.[87]

In case of a fire, the *case* of a scroll may be saved with the scroll, and the bag of phylacteries with them (even when the bag holds money also. They are taken into an alleyway which is not an open thoroughfare (that is, not a public domain).

One may save food for three meals, if a fire breaks out on Friday night; for two meals, if on Sabbath morning; and for one meal, if in the afternoon. A basketful of loaves may be saved even if it contains food for one hundred meals. The owner may invite others to save food for themselves; and they make their reckoning with him for compensation for their labor, after the Sabbath (if they wish to pay for their food), provided they did not help to be paid. The food is saved into a courtyard covered by an *eruv*.[88]

One may save his utensils and all the garments he can wear. He may return and save additional garments in like manner. A partition may be placed between the fire and the vessels, even if the latter are filled with water, and therefore could break and extinguish the fire.

A dish may be placed over a lamp, to keep it from scorching the rafters. A dish may also be placed over a scorpion (without committing a transgression in the category of hunting). In case of danger, one may even kill the scorpion.[89]

CHAPTER VI

Public and Personal Duties Superseding the Sabbath

THE DAY OF THE SABBATH is divinely fixed, but it was ordained for the preservation and enhancement of life; therefore, where the preservation and enhancement of life necessitates it, the Torah allows the setting aside of Sabbath observance, in cases where time is an essential element. The rabbis however, warned that the areas of Sabbath dispensation must not be extended beyond the absolutely necessary. "One must not say," states the *Mekhilta*, "that since we are allowed to work in the Temple we are also allowed to work outside the Temple."[1] Moreover, even in the Temple, only *kohanim* were allowed to perform the necessary work on the Sabbath. This is clearly implied in a Baraita which declares that a non-*kohen* who officiates on the Sabbath transgresses not only against the commandment forbidding a layman to officiate in the Temple, but also against the commandment forbidding work on the Sabbath.[2] According to Rabbi Yehudah ben Batira, the inhabitants in a besieged city must not say that since we are allowed to desecrate the Sabbath in part, that is in self-defense, we may desecrate it also in its entirety.[3]

1. Work Permitted in the Temple

In the Temple it was permitted to kindle a fire on the Sabbath, for the Torah says, "fire shall be kept burning on the altar, eternally" (Lev. 6:6), even on the Sabbath.[4] According to Rabbi Shimeon even the ashes of the altar were removed on the Sabbath.[5] From the verses, "Command the Children of Israel . . . to kindle an eternal light. . . . Aaron shall arange it from evening to morning, before God, eternally. . . ." (Lev. 24:2-4; Exod. 27:20, 21) the rabbis deduced that the *menorah* in the Tabernacle was lit on Sabbath, too.[6]

The two daily public sacrifices as well as those the Torah requires because of the Sabbath were offered on the Sabbath. The rabbis inferred this from the verse, "On the Sabbath (after) . . . the Sabbath offering . . . above the perpetual offering. . ."[7] (Numbers 28:19). One might venture the suggestion that this was done not only because it concerned the religious life of the community, but also because offering the daily public sacrifices as well as the additional ones for the Sabbath enhanced public worship on the Sabbath.

The fact that the Torah requires the offering of the two daily public sacrifices on the Sabbath was used by Hillel as a basis for the decision that the paschal lamb is offered on the Sabbath, as is related in the following story. Once, Passover began on Sunday, and the paschal sacrifice, therefore, had to be brought while it was still Sabbath (for it had to be offered before the end of the fourteenth, according to Numbers, ch. 12). The heads of the Sanhedrin, the Bnai Batira, did not know whether the paschal sacrifice superseded the Sabbath. The matter was finally referred to Hillel who ruled that it did. He reasoned as follows: The Torah requires that the paschal sacrifice be offered "in its due season" (*b'moado*) just as it requires that the public sacrifice (the *Tamid*) be offered "in its due season." This teaches us, Hillel reasoned, that just as the *Tamid* supersedes the Sabbath, so does the paschal sacrifice.[8]

Everything necessary to the offering of the paschal sacrifice, such as the slaughtering, the sprinkling of the blood, the cleansing of the bowels, and the offering of the fat, was permitted on the Sabbath, but the roasting of the lamb, and the offering of the bowels, which could be postponed till after the Sabbath, did not supersede it.[9]

Whether it was permissible to set aside the Sabbath in order to perform related functions that could have been performed before the Sabbath, such as bringing the lamb from outside the 2000 cubit limit (t'hum) (which is forbidden only by the rabbis), became a matter of dispute between Rabbi Akiva and Rabbi Eliezer, the latter permitting it; but Rabbi Akiva laid down the following rule: *Whatever can be done before the Sabbath does not supersede the Sabbath.*[10]

Permitted also on the Sabbath was the cereal offering (the initiation cakes) of the high priest, on the anniversary of his anointment.[11] The kneading, arrangement and baking of the cakes were done on the Sabbath, but not the grinding and sifting of the flour, in accordance with Rabbi Akiva's rule. The kneading and arrangement could not be done before the Sabbath because they had to be prepared and sanctified in a vessel which could not be kept overnight.[12] Their baking had to be done on the Sabbath because their name (tuphinim), in accordance with Rabbi Ishmael's interpretation, implies that they should be nice and fresh; or because the Torah commands that they "shall be made" (Lev. 6:16), implying even on the Sabbath.[13]

The *Omer* sacrifice and all its accessories, and the two loaves of bread (in the harvest offering) and their accessories, superseded the Sabbath. The *Omer* was cut on Friday night, when the sixteenth of Nisan occurred on the Sabbath, although it could have been cut before, because its ritual requires that it be cut not earlier than the second evening of Passover.[14] This was in accordance with the Pharisee teaching that the Torah's command to bring the *Omer* "on the morrow of the Sabbath" (Lev. 23:11) meant on the morrow of the day of rest, i.e., on the morrow of the first day of Passover, contrary to the Sadducees who interpreted it literally, that is, on the day after the Shabbat.[15]

Other *mitzvot* which superseded the Sabbath in the Temple were the *lulav* (on the first day of Succot), the willow (on the seventh day of Succot), the sending of the scapegoat to the wilderness (on Yom Kippur), the sounding of the *shofar* (on Rosh Hashanah and Yom Kippur) and the use of the musical instruments at the Temple services. According to Rabbi Eliezer, accessories also superseded the Sabbath.[16]

The following things did not supersede the Sabbath, because they could have been performed at other times: the *hagigah* or personal sacrifices brought on festivals, and the baking of the show bread.[17] *Generally, public sacrifices were permitted on the Sabbath and individual were not;* however, this rule had exceptions, as Rabbi Meir and Rabbi Yaakov pointed out. The ox sacrifice of Yom Kippur (*par shel Yom Hakippurim*), the cereal offering of the High Priest and the paschal sacrifice, although brought by individuals, superseded the Sabbath. The ox which a community offered when it forgetfully committed a sin (*par he-elem davar*), the sacrifices brought for idolatrous transgressions, and the festivals sacrifices (and the Sabbath sacrifices which failed to be offered on their designated day, for "once the day passes, its sacrifice ceases"), though public sacrifices, did not supersede the Sabbath. The Tosephta laid down this rule: Whatever has a definite time supersedes the Sabbath, even for an individual; whatever does not have a definite time, does not supersede the Sabbath, even for a community.[18]

2. Dispensations for the Community

The dates of the festivals are determined by the new

moons, that is, Rosh Hashanah occurs the first and second of the lunar month Tishre, etc. In the Temple, additional sacrifices (*musaph*) were offered on the first of every lunar month. In order to maintain the religious life of the community, it was, therefore, important that the new moon be ascertained. Before the discovery and formulation of the calendar system the new moon had to be sighted by reliable witnesses, who reported it to the *Sanhedrin* or chief religious court (*beit din*), and it proclaimed the new month. Sometimes the new moon was sighted by distant witnesses who had to desecrate the Sabbath in order to reach and report their evidence in time for the court to proclaim the new month before the first day passed. Since the continuity of the festival observance did not depend on every community, the witnesses were permitted to ride and perform other necessary tasks only in order to come and testify that they had sighted the new moon, but not to promulgate the court's proclamation.[19] After the destruction of the Second Temple, when sacrifices ceased, the religious leaders permitted the witnesses to desecrate the Sabbath only to testify concerning the months of Tishre and Nisan, for they were the months in which four of the major holidays occurred.[20] (Shevuot, occurring seven weeks after the first day of Passover, was necessarily determined by the first of Nisan.)

Witnesses were allowed to come from a distance, and to desecrate the Sabbath if necessary, even when the new moon could be seen clearly by all, so that they should not fail to come and testify on occasions when they think, erroneously, that others, too, can see the new moon, in which case the religious court would be unable to proclaim the new month.[21]

3. Dispensation for the Spiritual Life of the Individual

The Torah commands that circumcision be on the eighth day, and the rabbis interpreted it to mean even on the Sabbath. If there is any doubt about the need, as in the case of an hermaphrodite or if a child was born circumcised, or if there is any question about the day, as in the case of a child born at dusk (so that it is uncertain whether before or after sundown) then the circumcision may not take place on the Sabbath.[22]

Once Rabbi Yohanan was asked whether to circumcise on a Yom Kippur Sabbath a child, whose two brothers had died following circumcision, and he answered affirmatively.[23]

According to Rabbi Eliezer, everything connected with the circumcision may be done on the Sabbath. This includes even the cutting down of wood to make coal to forge the knife. But according to Rabbi Akiva, only that which could not have been done before the Sabbath, supersedes the Sabbath. The Talmud Yerushalmi (quoted by Rabbi Hananel) cites an incident where those in charge forgot to bring the knife on Friday, and two rabbis ruled that the knife could not be brought on the Sabbath (even through domains forbidden only by the rabbis); and the circumcision had to be postponed. An incident and the discussion in the Babylonian Talmud also implies that Rabbi Eliezer's opinion may not be followed even where only a rabbinic transgression is involved, for the opinion of Rabbi Eliezer, a member of the School of Shammai, was that of a minority, and hence not valid.[24]

4. Dispensation for the Physical Defense of a Community

Earlier we discussed the decision of Mattathias and his

followers to defend themselves on the Sabbath, lest they all be destroyed. The principle that self-defensive war is permissible on the Sabbath was later extended to non-defensive war begun before the Sabbath, and to the defense of individuals; but only work *directly* involved in the fighting or self-defense was permitted. The Tosephta states: Defenders of a city besieged by heathens, or those threatened by a rampaging river, or who are in a storm-tossed ship, or an individual pursued by robbers or evil spirits, may desecrate the Sabbath (to save themselves).[25] The Midrash relates that once the leaders of Sepphoris received, on the Sabbath, an evil request from the Roman government. They asked Rabbi Eliezer ben Prata what to do; and he, fearing to advise them openly to flee, replied suggestively, "Why do you ask me? Ask Jacob, Moses and David" (all of whom fled in time of danger). The leaders followed his suggestion, and fled.[26]

A town besieged may not meet the foe with weapons or desecrate the Sabbath, if the besiegers come only for money, for the Sabbath may be desecrated only if life is endangered. However, the people of a border city may desecrate the Sabbath even if the enemy comes only for money, because once he conquered the border city the enemy could conquer the rest of the land.[27]

In a non-defensive war, a heathen city must not be besieged less than three days before the Sabbath (during which time, supposedly, it could be conquered); but (according to Shammai) once the siege has started, it may be concluded, even on the Sabbath (for once started, victory becomes a matter of self-defense).[28]

According to Rabbi Yehoshua ben Levi, all dangerous animals may be killed on the Sabbath (in accordance with Rabbi Shimeon's opinion that work not needed *per se* is forbidden only by the rabbis, and where danger is involved the rabbis removed their restriction). A student once recited, "He who kills snakes and reptiles on the Sabbath displeases the pious." Rava bar Huna said to him, "And these pious displease the sages."[29]

5. Dispensation to Save Life

The principle that the preservation of life justifies the desecration of the Sabbath (pikuah nefesh doheh Shabbat) is fundamental to Judaism, and its acceptance must have followed the Maccabees' decision to defend themselves on the Sabbath. However, a basis for this universally (by then) accepted principle was still sought in the second century of the common era. The grounds proposed were legal and logical, as stated in the Mekhilta. Rabbi Ishmael reasoned thus: The Torah exempts a person who kills a thief in possible self-defense (Exod. 22:1). This exemption applies, by implication, also to one who kills in self-defense on the Sabbath. Surely, it should be permissible to desecrate the Sabbath in order to save a life.

Rabbi Eleazar ben Azariah reasoned that since it is permissible to desecrate the Sabbath to perform a circumcision, where only one organ is involved, it should surely be permitted to desecrate the Sabbath for the sake of the entire body (that is, to save a life). Rabbi Shimeon ben Menasia inferred from the Torah's teaching, "Keep the Sabbath, because it is holy to you. . . ." (Exod. 31:14), that "the Sabbath is handed over to you, and not you to the Sabbath." (This means that the Sabbath is for the physical and spiritual benefit of man.)

Rabbi Nathan deduced from the Torah's command, "And the Children of Israel shall keep the Sabbath," that you should make it possible for an Israelite to keep the Sabbath, for, "Desecrate for him (for one whose life is in danger) one Sabbath, so that he should be able to keep many Sabbaths."³⁰ The importance of the last point, which is probably implicit in all the other viewpoints, is evident from the following teaching by Rabbi Shimeon ben Eleazar: The Sabbath may be desecrated to save an infant one day old but not for the sake of a deceased King David, for as long as man lives he performs *mitzvot,* but when he dies his obligation to perform *mitzvot* ceases.³¹

Preservation of life is fundamental to Judaism, and therefore it permits the desecration of the Sabbath even where danger to life is only a possibility or doubtful *(safek nefashot)*.³² Thus, if one sees a child fall into a pit or locked in a room he may cut away the earth and break the door in order to save the child. The Gemara explains that the Sabbath is desecrated even where, in the case of the pit, the child may only be frightened, or where, in case the child is locked in, the grown up could sit outside and entertain the child. It is permissible to remove the debris of a collapsed structure in which a person was trapped, although it is not known whether he is alive. When the person is uncovered, if he is alive, everything may be done to save him, and he is cared for even if he will live only a short while; but if he is dead, nothing may be done for him on the Sabbath. One should zealously seek to save a life, and he need not consult a religious teacher for authority to desecrate the Sabbath.³³

Where saving a life is involved, one should desecrate the Sabbath, *immediately* and *personally,* even if the danger is not immediate. Thus, water may be heated for the dangerously sick even if the patient would most likely live till the following Sabbath; and the desecration need not be effected through non-Jews or minors but by adult Israelites. Anyone, including women and heathens, can declare a life in danger (and meriting Sabbath desecration). If two male Israelites declare a life not in danger and one Israelite supported by a woman or heathen declares it in danger, the latter opinion is followed (and the Sabbath may be desecrated). More than one Sabbath may be desecrated to save a life. Moreover, according to Rav, if a doctor diagnosed a sick man's condition as requiring treatment for eight days, the first of which begins on a Sabbath, the treatment is not postponed until after the Sabbath, but begun immediately, although two Sabbaths will thus be desecrated.[34]

Any ailment that possibly holds danger to life justifies the desecration of the Sabbath. These include pain in the throat, high fever, internal illness and a severe earache. Rav ruled that where life preservation is involved one should refrain from desecrating the Sabbath only where he is certain that the illness is not dangerous.[35]

Personal experience sometimes led the rabbis to include particular ailments among those justifying desecration of the Sabbath, as the following will illustrate. Rabbi Yehudah ruled that it is permissible to grind, carry and apply medicine for a bad eye. Rabbi Shmuel ben Yehudah ridiculed the ruling with the remark, "Who listens to Yehudah, desecrator of the Sabbath?" At a future time Rabbi Shmuel's eye pained him, and he sent to Rabbi Yehudah for permission to prepare and apply medicine. Rabbi Yehudah sent back this message: "For all it is permissible, but for you it is forbidden" (since he had refused to accept the decision before he was personally involved). Then Rabbi Yehudah explained that it was not *his* ruling, but his teacher Shmuel's (colleague of Rav). Shmuel's maid once had a bad eye, and although she cried, he paid no attention to her, which led to her losing the eye. Shmuel thereupon ruled that it is permissible to salve an eye "which rebels and wants to come out," for the eye is linked to the heart.[36]

Rav taught that ten persons who went to obtain the prescribed medicine, and who brought back ten times the necessary quantity, even for a patient who has already started to recover, are not regarded as transgressors. (Rabbenu Gershom explains: "For they all intended to help the sick, and we follow their intentions.")[37]

The Sabbath may be desecrated for a woman who is about to give birth. A midwife may be summoned for her from anywhere. If the woman needs a lamp, a neighbor may light it for her, even if the mother is blind, for the knowledge that those who help her have light reassures her. According to Rabbi Eliezer ben Azariah, the child may be washed also on the third day (regarded as critical) in water heated on the Sabbath.[38] Shmuel taught that it is permissible to operate during the Sabbath on a woman who died in childbirth, in order to remove the child, although there is no established indication (*hazakah*) that the child lives.[39]

The Sabbath may not be desecrated to mete out capital punishment.[40]

CHAPTER VII

The Sabbath in the Temple and the Synagogue

FROM ITS EARLY HISTORY, the Sabbath was a day not only of cessation from work and weekday routines, but also of blessing and sanctification. It became a day of worship and instruction as well as of joy and celebration. The earliest worship took place at the Tabernacle and Temple. On the Sabbath the daily public sacrifices were offered plus special ones for the Sabbath. According to the Book of Numbers (28:1-10), every day two flawless yearling male lambs were to be offered, one in the morning and the other at dusk, together with one tenth of an *ephah* of fine flour, mixed with a quarter of a *hien* of liquor (1½ liters) for each lamb. On the Sabbath the regular daily sacrifices were augmented by two additional flawless yearling male lambs, together with the required amounts of flour, oil and liquor. The Book of Chronicles (11, 8:12) tells us that Solomon offered sacrifices to God on the Sabbath, in accordance with the Torah of Moses.

Frequency and holiness of the sacrifices determined the order of the offering. Therefore, the daily sacrifices (*t'midim*) came first, then the additional ones for the Sabbath (*musaphim*) and last, those of the new moon (in case it occurred on a Sabbath). However, at the time of the sacrifices, the songs of the new moon (*Rosh Hodesh*) preceded those of the Sabbath, in order to publicize the new moon.[1]

The *Tamid* was slaughtered at half of the ninth hour

and offered at half of the tenth hour. On Passover eve it
was slaughtered at half of the eighth hour and offered at
half of the ninth hour, on Sabbath as well as on week days.
If Passover came on a Sabbath, the *Tamid* was slaughtered
at half of the seventh hour, and offered at half of the eighth,
and the paschal sacrifice after.[2]

Twenty-four watches (*mishmarot*) of *kohanim* served in
the Temple during the year, each twice a year, and each
watch was subdivided into units serving during the six days
of the week. On the Sabbath all members of the entire watch
served.[3] The members of the watches located in Jerusalem
used to pray that the sacrifices of their brothers be accepted.
In addition to the watches of *kohanim,* there were twenty-
four stations (*maamadot*) of Israelites, located in various
cities. These used to gather in the synagogues to fast and
pray. On Friday they did not fast, in honor of the Sabbath.
On Sundays they did not fast either, because the change from
Sabbath feasting to fasting might harm them, or because of
the Nazarenes. Gersonides explains that since the Nazarenes
regard Sunday as a holy day, they would be angry if the
people of the station fasted. According to Rabbi Samuel
Eliezer Eidels (*MaHaRSha*), Sunday was observed as a day
of rest in pre-Nazarene days. He explains that the members
of the *maamadot* did not fast on that day so that the heathens
should not misinterpret it as agreement by the Israelites
that Sunday was a holy day.[4]

According to Rabbi Shimeon ben Eliezer, indispensable
to the sacrifices were the *Kohanim* (who officiated), the
Levites (who sang), the Israelites (at their stations) and the
musical instruments.[5] On the Sabbath, the Levites recited
Psalm 92.[6] The high priest cut his hair every Friday, to
appear at his best before the watches, which were renewed
every Sabbath.[7]

There is a rabbinic dispute as to whether there was

instrumental music in the Temple on the Sabbath. The Gemara's conclusion, however, accords with the view of Rabbi Yirmeyahu, that music at the sacrifices was essential, and it superseded the Sabbath. (Moreover, instrumental music on the Sabbath is forbidden only by rabbinic decree.) At the sacrifices, the flutes played and the Levites sang before the altar, when the wine was poured for the morning and afternoon sacrifices.[8]

Every day in the Temple there were twenty-one sounds on the *shofar,* three for the opening of the gates, nine for the morning *Tamid,* and nine for the afternoon *Tamid.* When there was a *Musaph* offering, there were an additional nine sounds. On Friday there were an additional six, three to inform the people to stop working, and three to distinguish between the weekday and the Sabbath.[9]

The Book of Leviticus commands, "Take fine flour and bake twelve loaves of bread, each loaf two tenths of an *epha.* Arrange them into two settings (on which place frankincense), six in a setting, on the table of pure gold . . . every Sabbath day. Aaron and his sons shall eat (the bread) in a holy place." (Lev. 24:5-10). The rods on which the bread was placed were put into position before the Sabbath.[10]

On the first day of Succot, the palm branch ceremony was performed on the Sabbath, too. However, the people brought their palm branches on Friday, and on the Sabbath each took his own.[11] (The willows, for the ceremony on the seventh day, were also brought on Friday, as mentioned earlier.) The ceremony of pouring the water (*simchat beit hashoevah*) also took place on the Sabbath, but the water was put in the gold jug on Friday, and kept in the Temple court.[12]

Certain ceremonies which would have had to be observed on the Sabbath, according to their calendar, were either predated or postponed. Thus, if the fourteenth of Adar occurred on the Sabbath, the *megillah* was read before the Sabbath. If the date of those who had to bring the wood for the altar fire (*maarakhah*) fell on the Sabbath, the wood was brought later. The fasts, the *Hagigah* (the individual festival sacrifices), the *Hakhel* (the gathering of all people on the last day of Succot of the sabbatical year for the reading of the Book of Deuteronomy by the King, as commanded in Deut. 31:10-13) were all deferred to a weekday, if they occurred on the Sabbath.[13]

2. In the Synagogue

The Temple was a place of prayer and instruction as well as of sacrifices, as a number of biblical verses indicate.[14] However, it was the later contemporary and eventual successor of the Temple—the synagogue—which became the place of public worship and instruction, especially on the Sabbath. The Midrash states:

> The entire week Jews are occupied with their work, but on the Sabbath day they rise early and come to the synagogue, recite the *Sh'ma*, descend before the ark, read the Torah and conclude with a chapter from the Prophets (*haftarah*). God says to them, "My children, raise your voices, in order that the angels may hear you. Strive not to hate one another, not to be jealous, not to quarrel, and not to humiliate one another, in order to keep the angels" from denouncing you. . . . "Keep the Torah, in harmony."[15]

Another Midrash ascribes the study of Torah in the synagogue to the intentional example of Moses. Commenting on the verse, "And Moses assembled" (Exod. 35:1) the Midrash states, "God said 'Assemble large congregations and teach them the laws of the Sabbath, so that future generations will learn from you to assemble every Sabbath in the synagogue, there to teach the Children of Israel words of Torah, concerning the forbidden and permitted, and to praise My great name.' "[16]

Instruction or study in the synagogue consisted of readings from the Torah and Prophets (and in some localities also from the Holy Writings), with commentaries. The Torah, divided into weekly portions (*parshiot*) was completed annually in Babylonia, and triennially in Eretz Israel and Alexandria.[17] It was read during the Sabbath morning service, followed by a selection from the Prophets (*haftarah*), both of which were interpreted by designated persons. Some communities also had a selection from the Holy Writings at the Sabbath *Minha* service. Lectures on *Halakha* were delivered Sabbath afternoons, and probably on *Aggada*, on Friday evenings. The following laws and incident elaborate the above.

The reading from the scroll requires a quorum of ten, for rituals involving the sanctification of God's name (*davar shebik'dushah*) require such a quorum.[18]

Seven read from the Torah, and an eighth concludes (*Maftir*) with a reading from the Prophets; and for the honor of the Torah, he also repeats the last verses from the Torah. The reading is opened and closed with blessings. Formerly the blessings were pronounced by the first and last readers. Later it was instituted that all readers pronounce both blessings to prevent latecomers from thinking that there is no first blessing, and to keep early departers from thinking that there is no second blessing.[19]

Even women and children may be included among the seven readers; but the rabbis said that a woman must not read for the honor of the congregation. A barefooted (and also a sleeveless one, according to Rabbi Hananel) and a bareheaded man must not read in the Torah, for the honor of the congregation.[20] It is not quite clear what the Talmud means by discouraging reading by a woman "for the honor of the congregation," but from the context of the discussion of related laws (including the one that "an angry man" must not read "for the honor of the congregation") it seems that it means that a woman's status was not equal to that of a man (just as an Israelite's status was not equal to that of a *Kohen*), or that she was not as responsible as a man, and a congregation merits being read to by its highest or most responsible members.

For the sake of harmony, the *Kohen* reads first, then the Levite and third the Israelite. According to the School of Ishmael, the *Kohen* reads first, because the Torah teaches, "Sanctify him" (Lev. 21:8), the *Kohen*, to be first to read and to bless; and to prevent quarreling, he must not give up his right to another.[21] After the *Kohanim* come scholars who are also community leaders, then scholars fit to be leaders, then children of scholars who are leaders, then the heads of the congregation and then all others.[22]

He who opens the Torah looks into it, recites the blessings and then reads three verses, but he reads only one verse at a time to the interpreter so that the latter will make no mistake. In the Prophets, a reader takes three verses at a time, for even if the interpreter were to make a mistake, it would not affect ritual law. Prophetic selections need not be consecutive, but those from the Torah must, to keep the people from becoming confused.[23]

Only one person at a time may read the Torah, and only one may interpret (for, as explained by Rashi, the illiterates and women must hear clearly what is read and interpreted, so that they may understand the *mitzvot*). The selection from the Prophets (*haftarah*) is read by one and can be interpreted by two; but even ten may read *Hallel* and the *Megillah,* for since they are popular the people listen attentively.[24]

The reader is forbidden to help the interpreter, lest the people think that what he interprets is also written in the Torah.[25]

One person may read for all, in a city where only one knows how to read, but he sits down between readings. The three verses read by each are for the Torah, Prophets and Holy Writings.[26]

The *maftir* (the one who concludes) is given the honor of being the cantor, since he volunteered for something beneath his honor. According to Rabbi Shimi, he is allowed to be cantor in order to prevent a quarrel, for otherwise he might complain, "I should be *maftir,* and you cantor?" When the *maftir* is a minor, his father or his teacher is the cantor, for a minor may be a reader or translator, but he may not be the cantor or give the priestly blessing.[27]

When no translator and preacher are present, the *maftir* reads twenty-one verses, three for each of the required seven; otherwise, three verses are sufficient. Rabbi Shmuel bar Abba told that he was requested by Rabbi Yohanan to stop after reading ten verses, when a translator was present.[28]

According to Rabbi Yohanan, the greatest in the congregation rolls up the Torah, and he receives the reward of all.[29] The pure-minded (*n'kiei hadaat*) of Jerusalem used to follow the Torah when it was removed from, and returned to, the ark, to show their respect.[30]

There are four special Sabbaths during the seven weeks preceding Passover. The one immediately before or on *Rosh Hodesh Adar (Parshat Shekalim,* Exod. 30:11-16) was designated to inform the people to contribute their *shekels* during the month of Adar (the end of the fiscal year in Eretz Israel) for the Temple's public sacrifices. The Sabbath before Purim (*Parshat Zakhor*) was designated to remind the people about the command to eradicate Amalek (Deut. 25:17-19). The Sabbath after Purim (*Parshat Parah,* Num. ch. 19) was instituted to remind the people to purify themselves in preparation for the Passover (in which the unclean could not partake). The Sabbath before or on *Rosh Hodesh Nisan* (*Parshat Hahodesh,* Exod. 12:1-20) was designated for reading the laws concerning Passover.[31] The selections from the Prophets correspond to the Sabbath themes.

On Sabbath the Torah is also read at *Minha* services, and only three persons, without a *maftir,* are called, as on Mondays and Thursdays. Three are called up, according to Shmuel, for the three divisions of the TaNaKh (*Torah, Neviim, Ketuvim*). According to Rava, it is for the *Kohanim,* Levites and Israelites. At least ten verses are read, for the ten city 'idlers' (*batlanim*) needed to maintain a quorum for public worship (*minyan*). Another rabbi says the ten verses are for the Ten Commandments; and according to a third, they are for the ten expressions with which God created the world.[32]

In some communities there was a reading from the Prophets (*maftir*) at *Minha* services too; and in others a selection (*haftarah*) from the Holy Writings.[33]

During the Sabbaths of two months, Adar and Elul, the *Kallah* gatherings, for lay persons as well as for scholars, took place in Babylonia. (The derivation of the word *Kallah* is uncertain, one scholar deriving it from the Hebrew word for crown and another from the one for bride. It seems to us that it could have meant culmination, because of its timing and all-inclusiveness.) The rabbis sought to encourage attendance at the *Kallah* gatherings. Thus, one rabbi ruled that people who come to the *Kallah* on the Sabbath must not be given summons to appear in court after the Sabbath, so that they will not be frightened away from the lectures.[34] The Mishna also states that one may not read (for pleasure) from the Holy Writings, for that might keep him from attendance at the *Kallah* lecture which was devoted to a discussion of *Halakhah*.[35]

Lectures were delivered on Friday evenings, too, as is evident from remarkable story in which Rabbi Meir, in order to restore domestic peace, maneuvered to be spat upon by a member of his audience, a woman whose husband became angry because she had returned home from the lecture after the lamp had already burned out, and had requested to humiliate the lecturer—and the wife.[36]

"From Palestine," writes Harry Wolfson, "the custom of reading the Law on the Sabbath together with oral instruction in the form of a sermon or homily was brought over to Alexandria by the early Jewish settlers there. Philo himself has several references to this kind of instruction in the synagogue on the Sabbath."[37] In Philo's writings we find the following:

> Sabbath is the day on which God's perfect creation was revealed. The Torah forbids work to lighten from man his ceaseless labor and to refresh him. Physical labor is forbidden but not intellectual pursuits. One should occupy himself with philosophical study, for mental and spiritual perfection. On the Sabbath schools are open. People sit quietly and listen attentively because they are thirsting for words of wisdom. A very wise man lectures on a good and useful subject. . . . One sees that Moses does not allow the followers of his Torah to be idle even a moment. On the contrary, since we are made up of body and soul, he allots to each its necessary share, at the appropriate time.[38]

Philo's description of instruction in the synagogue of the Therapeutae of Alexandria may have applied, at least in part, also to the Palestinian and Babylonian synagogues. He writes:

> . . . Every seventh day they meet together for a general assembly, and sit in order, according to age. . . . The senior among them who has the fullest knowledge of the doctrines which they profess comes forward, and with visage and voice alike quiet and composed, gives a well reasoned and wise discourse. . . . This common sanctuary in which they meet every seventh day is a double enclosure, one portion set apart for the use of men, the other for women. For women, too, regularly make part of the audience with the same ardor and the same sense of calling. The wall between the two chambers rises up from the ground to three or four cubits. . . . This arrangement serves the modesty becoming to the female sex . . . and there is nothing to obstruct the voice of the speaker.[39]

3. Special Sabbath Prayers

Prayer is a personal duty (*hovat haguf*) and applies everywhere; nevertheless, since the Sabbath was inextricably linked with the synagogue, we shall discuss some of these special prayers in connection with the synagogue (bearing in mind that those who pray at home also recite these prayers).

When should one recite the Sabbath prayers? The rabbis differed, but the trend of opinion is that one may recite those of the Sabbath eve long before dark. Thus, Rabbi Hanina quotes Rabbi Ishmael ben Yose, who related: "Here my father prayed the Sabbath eve service before sunset." Rabbi Aha comments that although Rabbi Yohanan disagrees, Rabbi Yose's action was proper, for we should "take from the non-holy and add to the holy" (that is, we should begin observance of the Sabbath while it is still Friday). Another rabbi, Hanina ben Dosa, prayed so long before sunset that the donkey drivers were able to travel during the interval from the City of Arabia to Sepphoris. Another who prayed very early was Rav. Rabbi Yehudah Hanassi once mistook cloudiness for darkness, and after he prayed, the clouds lifted. He then went into the bath house (before the rabbinic prohibition), and when he came out he taught his students, but did not repeat the prayers.[40]

Although Rabbi Aha explains the permissibility of reciting Sabbath eve prayers early on the principle of taking from the non-holy and adding to the holy, other leading rabbis, including Rabbi Yehudah Hanassi, Rabbi Yose, Rabbi Yashia and Shmuel taught that it is permissible to recite all prayers early, including Saturday night's prayers while it is still Sabbath, and the *Kiddush* on Friday before dark and *Havdalla* on Saturday before dark.[41]

Rabbi Hanina used to robe himself on Sabbath eve and declaim: "Come, let us go to meet Sabbath the queen." Rabbi Yannai, after robing himself, used to say, "Welcome, O bride, welcome, O bride."[42]

Rav taught that even when one prays by himself he should recite the *Vayekhulu* (the passage in Gen. 2:1-3).[43]

According to Rava, a cantor need not refer to the festival occurring on a Sabbath when he repeats part of the *Amidah* (*m'ein shevah*) at the evening service, for if not for the Sabbath, there would be no repetition. Rashi explains that in talmudic days the synagogues were located far from the homes. On weekdays the people prayed at home, after the completion of their work. On Friday evenings they came to the synagogues, but some arrived late. For their benefit, the service was lengthened by means of the partial repetition of the *Amidah*. Since it was done because of the Sabbath, there was no reference in it to the festival.[44]

According to Rav, people who recite the *Kiddush* in the synagogue need not recite it again at home for themselves, but only for their family.[45] But according to Shmuel, the *mitzvah* of *Kiddush* may be fulfilled only at home, except for guests who eat and sleep in the synagogue, for *Kiddush* must be recited where the meal is eaten.[46]

At the morning service of a Sabbath *Rosh Hodesh*, the *maftir* does not refer to *Rosh Hodesh* in his blessings, for if not for Sabbath there would be no reading from the Prophets. At the *Minha* services of a festival occurring on a Sabbath, in localities having a reading from the Prophets (*haftarah*), the *maftir* does not refer to the festival, for if not for the Sabbath there would be no *haftarah* at *Minha*. On the other hand, reference is made to the Sabbath, even at the *Neila* services of Yom Kippur which are held entirely because of Yom Kippur.[47]

A *Kohen* with a hand defect must not pronounce the priestly blessings, for the people are tempted to look at him, despite the prohibition. The Gemara explains that the *Sh'khinah* rests upon the *Kohanim* during their blessing of the people, and looking at the *Kohanim* then might cause one's eyes to grow dull. However, Tosafot quotes the Talmud Yerushalmi that looking at the *Kohanim* leads to distraction during the prayers.[48] The people of Beit Shean, Beit Haifa and Tivonin must not officiate as cantors because they do not distinguish between the *aleph* and *ayin*.[49]

CHAPTER VIII

Positive Observance in the Home

*"And God blessed the seventh day . . ." with the light
of man's face; the light of man's face on the Sabbath
is different from at other times.*

(Rabbah, Genesis, 11:2)

*Said R. Shimon ben Lakish, on Sabbath eve God
places in man an excessive soul (n'shamah y'teirah),
and at the end of Sabbath it is taken from him.*

(Beitza, 16a)

THE SABBATH, like a dear and most welcome guest, is
prepared for with much anticipation. She (*she,* for Sabbath
is both queen and bride) is ushered in and out with great
ceremony, and is enjoyed fully during her stay. One works
the entire week in order to be able to enjoy her presence;
and one works the entire week in order not to have to desecrate her holiness. Rabbi Akiva says, ". . . One who idles
away the week does not have what to eat on the Sabbath."
Rabbi Dostai, in commenting on the verse, "Six days you
shall work, and on the seventh day you shall rest" (Exod.
23:12) stated, "One who does not work during the six will
have to work on the seventh. Because he did not work, he
may have to become a mercenary, and may have to desecrate
the Sabbath."[1] In order to express the idea that after this
world (or life) it will be too late for nations (or individuals)
to do good in order to receive reward, the Talmud has God
exclaim, "Foolish people, he who toils on the eve of the
Sabbath has what to eat on the Sabbath, but he who did
not toil, what shall he eat?"[2]

89

According to some rabbis, the actual preparation should commence long before the advent of the Sabbath. Thus, the Talmud tells, Shammai the Elder used to live his entire life in honor of the Sabbath. When he found a choice animal, he kept it for the Sabbath. Then, if he found a still nicer one, he kept that one for the Sabbath. However, all of the deeds of Hillel the Elder, (those of the weekdays, too) were for the sake of God, in the spirit of Psalms (68:20), "Blessed be the Lord every day."[3] Rabbi Simlai taught, "Remember the Sabbath day" (Exod. 20:8), before it comes, and "Keep it" (Deut. 5:12), when it comes. If you find something desirable, prepare it for the Sabbath. Rabbi Tanhuma related that once, while they were dining in the home of Abbahu, dates were served, and Rabbi Abbahu requested that they be kept for the Sabbath. One should sanctify the Sabbath with food and clean garments. Therefore, Rabbi Hanan taught, a man should have two cloaks, one for weekdays and one for the Sabbath.[4]

Rabbi Huna was concerned that others have vegetables for the Sabbath. On Sabbath eve he used to send his servant to the market (shuk), to buy up every vegetable left, and then he dumped them into the river. His motivation is explained in the following questions and answers in the Talmud:

"Why did he not give it to the poor?"

"Lest they depend on him, and not buy the vegetables themselves anymore."

"Why, then, did he buy them altogether?"

"So that the gardeners continue to bring their vegetables (to the shuk)."[5]

Another Rabbi, Hanina, used to send four zuzim to a poor man every Friday.[6] Rabbi Eleazar ben Shimeon encouraged people to borrow for the Sabbath, by declaring in behalf of God, "Children, borrow in My name, so that you will be able to keep the holiness of the day, and have faith that I will repay you." Another rabbi states that a man's food for the entire year is determined during the Days of Judgment; but his expenditures for his Sabbath, festivals and children's education are not predetermined. (He is repaid what he expends.) Although Rabbi Akiva taught that a man should prepare on the Sabbath no more than on a weekday rather than depend on other human beings, nevertheless, one should prepare something special for the Sabbath.[7]

A man should personally help prepare for the Sabbath, as indicated by the following teachings and laws. Elijah will not come (to herald the coming of Messiah) on the eve of the Sabbath or festivals in order not to interfere with preparations for the holy days.[8] A man is not given a summons to court on the eve of the Sabbath, even to appear *after* the Sabbath, in order not to interfere with his preparation for the Sabbath.[9] One should not travel on Friday more than three *parsas*, so that he should have time to prepare and rest for the Sabbath.[10] Some rabbis, like Rabbi Nahman bar Itzhak, used to help personally in bringing in the Sabbath supplies on Friday.[11] Rava taught that "He who is overhasty is a sinner" (Proverbs 19:2) refers to one who sends to his wife, on Friday, meat not cleaned of its veins and fat, for the women are busy, and might not remove the veins, and the husband would be responsible.[12]

"As a rose is used in the preparation for the Sabbath," says the Midrash, "so is Israel prepared for the coming redemption."[13] The Talmud tells that Rabbi Shimeon ben Yohai and his son Rabbi Eleazar saw an old man running, with two myrtles in his hands one Friday. They asked him, "What are these for?" and he answered, "In honor of the Sabbath." Then they asked him, "Is one not enough?" And he explained that one is for *Zakhor* and the other for *Shamor*

(the two different words beginning the fourth commandment in Exodus and Deuteronomy). Rabbi Shimeon then
remarked to his son, "See how precious the *mitzvot* are to
the Jewish people."[14] In connection with this incident it is
apropos to cite an interesting law. In the collision of two
persons on a thoroughfare, with mutual injury as the consequence, the law is that the person who was running is liable.
However, Eisi ben Yehudah taught that a man who is running on Friday toward evening is not liable, for he has permission to run, to receive the Sabbath.[15]

After one has prepared his food and other needs, he has
to prepare himself by washing up, as is evident from the
story about the two men who wagered concerning Hillel's
self-control. The man who believed he could anger Hillel
chose Friday afternoon, when the rabbi was washing his head,
in order to achieve his victory.[16] Rabbi Yehudah bar Elai
used to wash his hands and feet in a basin of hot water, and
then he robed himself in his linen cloak, with *tzitzit*, "and
he looked like an angel of God."[17] Rabbi Meir sought to
get his neighbors into the proper mood for the reception of
the Sabbath. They used to quarrel every Friday (probably
about Sabbath preparations, or because their nerves were
tense as a consequence of the preparations or lack of supplies). On three occasions Rabbi Meir interceded, until he
got his neighbors out of the habit of quarreling.[18]

As pointed out in an earlier section, one may do what
will help to retain but not to increase the warmth of the
food prepared for the Sabbath. Thus, according to the
Mishna, food may be set on a stove heated with stubble or
straw on the eve of the Sabbath; but if it was heated with
peat or wood, one must first sweep out the coal or cover
it with ashes, lest he will come to rake it, in order to hasten
the cooking.[19]

Pots may be covered with hides, which may be handled; and with wool shearings which may not be handled (but one removes the lid and lets them fall off). If the shearings are not kept for weaving but for covering, they may be handled. The food may be covered before the Sabbath, but not during the Sabbath, even with materials that only help retain the heat, lest he will forgetfully reheat the food on the fire when he finds that it has cooled.[20]

2. *Eruvin*

The *eruv* (literally, 'blending' of—area or time) was a means evolved to facilitate mobility on the Sabbath, and preparation for the Sabbath when it is preceded by a festival. Although a legal fiction (according to Dr. Solomon Zeitlin), it was necessary, and compatible with the basic Sabbath laws. The rabbis praised it, and even ascribed its origin to King Solomon.[21]

The spatial *eruvin* were established in order to allow one 1) to walk beyond the two-thousand cubit limit, 2) to carry from private domain to public domain, and 3) to carry from house to house within a courtyard. Thus, a person who finds himself outside his city, more than two-thousand cubits away, when it is almost Sabbath, may *declare his resting place* at the base of a tree which he recognizes. He then has two thousand cubits to the tree, and two thousand cubits from the tree to his house. A person not on the road, who wants to go outside his city in order to welcome his teacher on the Sabbath, may establish his *eruv* either by walking on Friday, to a point within two thousand cubits of his permanent residence or by having his bread placed there. (He establishes residence where his bread is.) He then has two thousand cubits from his temporary residence. The messenger whom he designates to carry his bread and establish his residence must be one who believes in the idea of the *eruv*. All food (excluding water and salt) can be used. Neighbors in a courtyard "blend" their homes by contributing food which is placed in one of the homes, making them all appear as tenants of the house and as having one domain.[22]

The 2000 cubit limit which a person has from his resting place or city is rabbinic, and the restriction is therefore alleviated where possible. This is illustrated in the following incident related in the Talmud. One Friday afternoon, it became dark before Rabbi Hoshaya's daughter-in-law returned home from the bathhouse. Her mother-in-law thereupon made an *eruv* for her by sending food to within 2000 cubits from her home, so that her daughter-in-law had that additional permissible distance in which to walk. The question came before Hiyya, and he declared the *eruv* invalid; but he was reprimanded by Rabbi Ishmael ben Yose who told him, "Babylonians, why are you so strict where *eruvin* are concerned? My father taught that we seek to alleviate in matters of *eruvin*."[23]

To establish a partnership in an alleyway (*shitufei mavuiot*) its neighbors place some fruit or wine or oil in a jug which is left in the alley. One person may contribute all the food, but he must transmit to the others, through a designated Israelite, rights to the food, with the knowledge of all participants.[24]

A public thoroughfare can be covered by an *eruv* by placing the form of a door on one end and a board or rafter on the other end.[25] A city with only one entrance may be covered by an *eruv* in a similar way.[26]

The covering of a courtyard by an *eruv* (*eruvei hatzerot*) was not required by law, but it was instituted only to keep the law of *eruvei t'humin* from being forgotten by children.

According to the Talmud Yerushalmi, it was to foster friendship among neighbors.[27]

Another type of *eruv,* permitting otherwise forbidden food preparation for the Sabbath during a festival occurring on a Friday, was instituted to keep the Sabbath from being ignored, because of the preoccupation with the festival. Thus, one prepares a dish on the eve of the festival as an *eruv,* and this becomes the basis for the permission to cook during the festival for the Sabbath.[28] Shmuel's father used to make an *eruv* for the entire city of Nehardea. Rabbi Ami and Rabbi Assi made an *eruv* for all the inhabitants of Tiberias.[29]

According to the Babylonian Talmud one who works after *Minha* on the eve of Sabbath and festivals will not realize any blessing in his work.[30] But according to the Talmud Yerushalmi one may work "six days" until the sun sets.[31]

One should examine his pockets on Friday afternoon lest he forget and go out with something in them to the *r'shut harabim.*[32]

If the fourteenth of Nisan occurs on a Sabbath, all *hametz* except food for two meals, has to be removed by the end of Friday.[33]

Sabbath observance is, of course, an individual responsibility; but the community seeks to enforce or encourage public adherence (as we shall see later), and it reminds its members to lay aside their work and complete preparations for the Sabbath. Thus, the School of Rabbi Ishmael taught that six *shofar* sounds are blown on the eve of the Sabbath: the first to remind the field workers to stop working; the second to remind city workers and shopkeepers; the third as a reminder to light candles, according to Rabbi Nathan, and according to Rabbi Yehudah Hanassi it is to remind the men to remove their *tefillin*. After a pause long enough to broil a small fish, three more sounds are blown to distinguish between the non-holy and holy (the weekday and the Sabbath). The field workers close to the city wait for those farther away so that they may all enter the city together and no one will be suspected of working after the sounding of the *shofar*. After the third sounding, housewives either remove their hot dishes from the stove or, if they intend to keep their dishes on the stove, put ashes on the coal, and then they light candles. The sexton who sounds the *shofar* puts it away in a designated place on the roof of the synagogue, for after the Sabbath has begun, he may not handle the *shofar* (since it is not used on the Sabbath it is *muktzah*).[34] Even on a festival Friday there is the sounding of the *shofar*, but the routine is somewhat different.[35]

Josephus tells that a priest blew the *shofar* before the commencement of the Sabbath, to remind people to stop working, and at the end of the Sabbath, to inform them that they may start work again.[36]

According to Rabbi Yehoshua ben Levi, one must not eat when the time for *Minha* has arrived until he has prayed.[37] If Tisha b'Av comes on a Sabbath or Sunday one may eat on the Sabbath. If it occurs on Friday, one may eat before dark food equivalent to the bulk of an egg, so that he should not enter the Sabbath suffering hunger. Rabbi Yehudah told that Rabbi Akiva once gave his students a practical demonstration of this law by personally sipping a soft-boiled egg without salt.[38]

Workers and professionals must put away their tools before dark lest they forget and go out with them to the *r'shut harabim* after dark. Thus, a tailor must not go out with his needle toward dark, lest forgetfully he will carry it into the *r'shut harabim* after dark, nor may a scribe go out with his pen toward dark, for the same reason.[39]

Preparation for the Sabbath should include making the beds and setting the table. The table should be set, Rabbi Eliezer taught, even if one needs no more food than the bulk of an olive.[40] Then one should give his family, gently, three reminders, in the following words: "Have you tithed? Have you prepared an *eruv* (for the courtyard)?" and, "Light the candles."[41] The lighting of the candles, signifying the beginning of the Sabbath, should be done sometime before the Sabbath, because, as Rabbi Ishmael taught, the Torah (in connection with Yom Kippur) commands that we take from the non-holy and add to the holy.[42]

Some sectarian groups interpreted the verse, "Do not kindle a fire" (Exod. 35:3) to mean that the enjoyment of fire is also forbidden. The rabbinic position is that the enjoyment of fire ignited before the Sabbath is permitted, and that not only is it permissible to light candles for the Sabbath but that it is also praiseworthy, and according to many rabbis even mandatory. The Torah teaches, the *Mekhilta* says, that we must not kindle a fire on the Sabbath, but it is permissible to kindle it on the eve of the Sabbath for the Sabbath. Therefore, it is permissible to enjoy candles lit before the Sabbath and to keep food warm.[43]

Our rabbis sought to encourage the lighting of candles on the eve of Sabbath, for the sake of domestic harmony as well as for the enjoyment of the Sabbath.

The glory of the Sabbath, says the Midrash, is enhanced by its candles. God says, "If you keep the Sabbath candles, I will enable you to see the light of Zion."[44] Rabbi Abbahu interpreted the verse "And I have been robbed of peace" (Lamentations 3:17) as referring to the inability to light

Sabbath candles.[45] Rav taught that washing the hands and feet on the eve of Sabbath is optional, but lighting candles is obligatory (hova).[46] Rabbi Huna taught that he who lights candles regularly will have children who are scholars.[47] (They will study on Sabbath evenings.)

The importance of the Sabbath candles is evident from the following laws: One who has to choose, financially, between Sabbath and Hanukah candles should purchase the former, for the sake of domestic peace (for, Rashi explains, people find it painful to sit in darkness). One who cannot afford both Kiddush wine and Sabbath candles should buy the candles, for family harmony. On the other hand, one who is unable to buy Kiddush wine and Hanukah candles should buy the latter, in order to publicize the miracle.[48]

If one can afford it, he should light more than one lamp, and use a measure of oil sufficient to last into the night. Thus, Rabbi Eleazer told that once he lit his lamp on the eve of the Sabbath, and it burned until the end of the Sabbath. Rabbi Abin Nagra used to light many candles.[49]

As a home ceremony it was natural for candle lighting to become the woman's responsibility. However, says the Talmud Yerushalmi, the mitzvah was given to woman because she (Eve) caused the light (soul) of man (Adam) to go out.[50]

Rabbi Joseph's wife used to light candles when it was almost dark. After he told her that she must do it earlier, she wanted to light them very early. He then quoted her a baraita which states that one must not light candles too early or too late. Shmuel said that one star means that it is still day, two that it is dusk, and three that it is already night.[51]

As candle lighting became an important aspect of Sabbath observance, it became necessary to decide what materials may be used, and how. The first criterion for both was the prevention of Sabbath desecration. Some rabbis believed also that the materials should be compatible with the spirit of the Sabbath. Others, however, held that one may use any materials he can obtain, except those likely to cause desecration.

According to the Mishna, wicks may not be made of raw silk or cedar-fibre or other materials that do not take hold of the flame.[52] Oils and greases that do not stick to the wick, causing the lamp to go out, may not be used. Balsam may not be used because it is volatile, and also lest one will take from it. Rabbi Tarphon says only olive oil may be used. Rabbi Yohanan ben Nuri disputed this, saying, What shall the Babylonian Jews, who have only sesame oil, do? And the Median who have only nut oil? And the Capadocians who have only naphtha oil? Therefore, all oils (except those that might cause one to desecrate the Sabbath) may be used.[53]

One may not place a perforated egg shell, filled with oil, at the mouth of a lamp, so that the oil drip into the lamp, lest he will come to take from the oil, which is *muktzah*. However, if the vessel dripping the oil and the lamp were joined by the potter it is permissible, for the two are one vessel.[54]

The Sabbath evening prayers should be recited at the beginning of the Sabbath, and they should be followed by the recitation of the *Kiddush* (proclaiming the sanctity of the day), which is associated by the rabbis with wine. ". . . To sanctify it," says the *Mekhilta*, means "with a blessing; declare the holiness of the day, at its beginning, over wine."[55] The Talmud extends this interpretation as follows: " 'Remember the Sabbath Day to sanctify it'; remember it over wine upon its entry, in the evening, and by day."[56]

According to Rav, the wine for *Kiddush* must be of a quality fit for the altar. Therefore, malodorous wine may not be used, for, "Bring it to your ruler, will he receive you graciously?" (Malachi 1:8). Nevertheless, when Rav preferred bread, he recited the *Kiddush* over it.[57]

According to Beit Shammai one first recites the blessing for the Sabbath and then the one for the wine, for without the Sabbath there would be no *Kiddush*. But according to Beit Hillel the blessing for the wine comes first, for the *Kiddush* is recited over wine; and also because the blessing over the wine is recited at all times, and being regular it precedes the occasional.[58] On a Sabbath festival, the elders of Pumbedita used to conclude the *Kiddush* with the words, "He Who sanctifies the Sabbath, Israel and the seasons," placing the Sabbath first, for the Sabbath is fixed; but the festival dates are declared by Israel (the religious court).[59]

One should not eat on the eve of the Sabbath and festivals after *minha* so that he should enter the Sabbath craving food.[60]

The tray with the food is brought in after the *Kiddush*, in honor of the Sabbath. If it is more practical to bring in the tray before the recitation of the *Kiddush*, then it is covered with a cloth during the *Kiddush*.[61] Rabbi Abba taught that on the Sabbath one should pronounce the blessing over two loaves of bread. According to Rabbi Zerika one should have three meals during the Sabbath, but according to Rabbi Hidka he should have four meals.[62] A poor transient is investigated if he requests clothing but not if he requests food. On the Sabbath he is provided with three meals.[63] The food should be as abundant and good as one can afford. If possible, one should have white bread covered with honey and oil; and vegetables, large fish and garlic heads.[64] According to Rav, any little thing prepared especially in honor of the Sabbath is regarded as Sabbath joy.[65] One should prepare his Sabbath meal with greater care so that it be as tasty and fragrant as possible.[66]

One should allow his animal to graze on the Sabbath.[67] In accordance with Rabbi Meir's teaching that a person should recite one hundred blessings daily, one should on the Sabbath (when the *Amidah* does not have eighteen blessings) complete the number over spices and delicacies.[68]

According to Rabbi Yehudah Hanassi, one should sanctify the Sabbath by wearing his best clothes. According to Rabbi Hanina it is enough if he changes some clothes in honor of the Sabbath. Abin bar Hasdai says he should lower his garments.[69]

Most rabbis agree that the Sabbath is a time for relaxation and physical enjoyment as well as for worship, meditation and study. Nevertheless, there seems to be a prevailing view that scholars who toil over their studies the entire week should enjoy themselves on the Sabbath; and laborers who are occupied the entire week with their work should study Torah on the Sabbath.[70]

Despite some contrary opinions, the talmudic view is that all things of physical enjoyment such as eating, drinking, washing, anointing, wearing of shoes, and cohabitation, fit into the pattern of Sabbath observance. According to Shmuel, a scholar's cohabitation time is Friday night.[71] If one vows not to receive favors from those who keep the Sabbath, he may not receive anything from Jews and Samaritans. If he vows not to receive favors from those who eat garlic, he may not receive favors from Jews and Samaritans, who eat it on Friday evenings, in order to increase fertility.[72]

On the Sabbath one should feel as if his *entire* work were done.[73] Therefore, it is forbidden to visit one's field on the Sabbath, to ascertain its needs. It is even forbidden to pray for one's personal needs on the Sabbath. However, it is permitted to discuss community matters, even in such public places as theaters and circus arenas. Hence, the betrothal of girls and the learning of a trade by children may be arranged on the Sabbath, according to Beit Hillel. One may also visit the sick and console mourners on the Sabbath.[74]

A congregation whose members suffered a great loss in the fall of the price of fine garments, may pray for a price rise even on the Sabbath.[75]

The prevailing rabbinic views is that mourning is not compatible with the spirit of the Sabbath. On the Sabbath the mourner may eat meat, drink wine, and do all things permitted to non-mourners. However, Sabbath is counted as a day of mourning.[76] It is also permissible to greet mourners on the Sabbath, where it is customary.[77]

One may cut his hair on Thursday in honor of the Sabbath, and if he failed to cut it then he may do so on Friday afternoon, even when Tisha b'Av comes on a Friday.[78]

A man who vowed not to eat the entire year may have it annulled by being asked whether he vowed to fast also on the Sabbath and festivals. At first the sages said that the vow is nullified only for the Sabbath and festivals. Later Rabbi Akiva taught that if the vow is partially nullified it becomes completely null.[79]

Because the Sabbath is itself a sign and a reminder of God, one does not on the Sabbath, put on phylacteries (*tefillin*) which the Torah (Exod. 13:9) commands as a sign. Moreover, the symbolic power of the Sabbath is even greater than that of the phylacteries, for the Sabbath is also called a reminder of the covenant (*brit*) between God and Israel.[80] Nevertheless, the Sabbath has only symbolic, derivative holiness but no intrinsic divine power. Therefore, a mourner who rent his garment on the Sabbath has fulfilled the *mitzvah* of *kriah;* and one who carried on the Sabbath *matzah* from the public domain to his house, where he eats it, has fulfilled the command to eat *matzah* on the first day of Passover; and an animal which was slaughtered on the Sabbath is kosher.[81]

The Sabbath is a day of complete rest and peace; and it should not be disturbed by dispensable noise or speech. An extreme case of such observance is that of Rabbi Eila, who returned late from the *beit hamidrash* one Friday night and slept on the ladder, not wishing to awaken his sleeping household by knocking on the door.[82] However, Rava told Rabbi Ulla, who once became angry at a man who knocked on the door because "he desecrates the Sabbath," that "only the sound of music is forbidden" on the Sabbath.[83] When the mother of Rabbi Shimeon bar Yohai spoke unnecessary words on the Sabbath, he used to say, "Mother, it is Sabbath today," and she became quiet.[84] The rabbis looked askance even at the teaching of Torah when it, or its material reward, did not accord with the spirit of the Sabbath. Thus, they teach that among the four persons who see no sign of blessing in their earnings is the lecture interpreter, because his compensation appears like Sabbath pay.[85] A father may not teach his children how to read for the first time on the Sabbath, because it deprives him of the leisure for the enjoyment of the Sabbath; or because the abundant Sabbath food makes the strain of initial teaching potentially harmful, in accordance with Shmuel's principle that "a change in routine is the beginning of stomach trouble."[86]

The positive observance of the Sabbath in the home (and in the synagogue and elsewhere) includes all aspects of living, from dressing, eating and walking, to thinking, talking, studying and worshipping, and even attitudes and feeling. This is summed up in a *Mekhilta* commentary on the verse,

"Therefore God blessed the day of the Sabbath and sanctified it" (Exod. 20:11). He blessed it with *manna*, and sanctified it with *manna*, according to Rabbi Ishmael. Rabbi Akiva says, He blessed with *manna*, and sanctified it with a blessing. Rabbi Itzhak says, He blessed it with the *manna* and sanctified it with the wood-gatherer. Rabbi Shimeon bar Yohai says, He blessed it with *manna*, and sanctified it with the light of Sabbath. Rabbi Shimeon ben Yehudah of Acco says, He blessed it with *manna*, and sanctified it with the light of man's face (which differs on the Sabbath from the weekdays).[87]

All the rabbis agree that preparation for the Sabbath, abstention from work, and physical enjoyment are essential aspects of the Sabbath blessing. They differ in their emphases on the aspects of sanctification. To Rabbi Ishmael, the preparation before the Sabbath and the freeing of oneself from routine on the Sabbath, makes the day distinct and holy. To Rabbi Akiva, the blessings and worship on the Sabbath create an atmosphere of holiness. To Rabbi Itzhak, awareness of the Sabbath strictness (with desecration entailing severe punishment—signifying degrees of sanctity) constitutes the holiness. To Rabbi Shimeon bar Yohai it is the Sabbath ritual and cheer. And to Rabbi Shimeon ben Yehudah it is the spiritual joy that radiates on the Sabbath.

The *havdalla*, the ceremony for distinguishing the Sabbath from the weekdays, preferably should be recited over wine.[88] The order of the service, according to Beit Hillel, is: wine, spices, light and *havdalla* (the declaration of the distinction). One should perform the *havdalla* ceremony although a prayer declaring the distinction is included in the *amidah* service.[89] According to Rava, the order of the service, when a festival comes at the end of a Sabbath, is: wine, *kiddush* (declaring the holiness of the day), light, *havdalla* and season (*YaKNaHZ*). The *havdalla* is not mentioned first, not to make the holiness of the Sabbath appear like a burden.[90]

A torch is preferable for the *havdalla* light.[91]

The candle must be enjoyed, and therefore must be close enough to distinguish by its light between two coins.

A lamp which burned from before the Sabbath eve may be used for the *havdalla*. If it was lit during the Sabbath for a sick person, it may also be used.[92]

When the *havdalla* light is brought into the synagogue, each one in the congregation recites a blessing, in order not to interrupt the study, according to Beit Shammai. But according to Beit Hillel, one person recites the blessing for all, "for the king's glory is in the multitude of people."[93]

The blessing over the light is said at the end of the Sabbath and Yom Kippur, according to Rabbi Yohanan, since on those days one is unable to light a candle.[94]

In the *havdalla* one refers to these distinctions: between light and darkness, Israel and the nations and the seventh day and the non-holy days; and, says Shmuel, one concludes with the words: "He Who distinguishes between the holy and non-holy."[95]

One inaugurates the Sabbath before sundown, to show his love; and he ushers it out after sundown, not to make it appear like a burden.[96] One who did not recite the *havdalla* on Saturday night may do it until Wednesday.[97] However, according to Rabbi Eliezer ben Yaakov, one must not begin his work until he has recited the *havdalla*.[98]

According to Rabbi Hanina, one should set his table at the conclusion of the Sabbath. It is comparable to a farewell banquet for a departing royal guest.[99]

In a mixed city of Jews and non-Jews the public bathhouse may be used by the Jews as soon as the Sabbath is over. However, if the majority of the inhabitants are Jews one must not use the bathhouse before the time that it would take to heat it up after the Sabbath.[100]

CHAPTER IX

Enforcement and Encouragement of Sabbath Observance

> *R. Shimon ben Lakish says, God declares, "My chil-*
> *dren, work six days for yourselves, and one with Me."*
> (Pesikta 23:2).

> *"Better is a handful with satisfaction than two hand-*
> *fuls with trouble and striving after the wind," means*
> *the day of the Sabbath is better than the six days of*
> *work. . . . Israel will be redeemed by merit of keeping*
> *the Sabbath.*
> (Rabbah, Kohelet, 4).

> *"Happy is the man who does this . . . who keeps the*
> *Sabbath from desecrating it. . . ." (Isaiah 56); He*
> *who keeps the Sabbath is kept far from sin.*
> (*Mekhilta,* Vayassa 6; Exod. 16:28).

IN HIS COMMENTARY on the verse, "Keep My commandments. . . . I am the Lord" (Lev. 19:30), Nahmanides
states: "The Torah warnings against the desecration of the
Sabbath are numerous, as they are (numerous) against
idolatry, because the Sabbath, too, is equivalent to all the
mitzvot, for he who does not keep the Sabbath denies
creation by God. . . ."

The Torah decrees death for four categories of transgression, for the three cardinal sins of idolatry, adultery
and murder, and for Sabbath desecration.[1] In decreeing
death for Sabbath desecration, it states, "Keep the Sabbath,
because it is holy unto you; those that desecrate it shall be

106

put to death; for whoever does work on it, that person shall be cut off from his people" (Exod. 31:14, 16).[2] In Numbers, however, we are told that the wood gatherer was stoned to death. (Num. 15:32-36). According to the *Mekhilta,* Exodus 31 refers to one who transgresses knowingly, but without warning by witnesses.[3] Numbers refers to one who transgresses after having been duly warned that doing his particular work (one of the thirty-nine categories forbidden by the Torah) on the Sabbath will make him subject to capital punishment.[4] According to Rabbi Yehudah, the transgressor must also be told by the witnesses the manner in which he would be put to death if he should transgress.[5]

Generally the death penalty was meted out only to those who committed transgressions within the thirty-nine categories of work forbidden by the Torah. However, in time of religious persecution, when an example of laxity could inspire more serious transgressions, the death penalty was given even for transgression of rabbinic prohibitions.[6]

The rabbis sought to limit in every possible way the instances in which the death penalty was given. Thus, according to Rabbi Yose, the Torah specifies "Do not kindle a fire in your dwelling places on the Sabbath" (Exod. 35:3), to teach that there is no capital punishment for making a fire on the Sabbath.[7] And according to Rabbi Akiva there is no death for one who travels beyond the Sabbath day journey limit, although according to Rabbi Akiva it is forbidden by the Torah.[8] Like other capital punishment cases, those concerning Sabbath desecration, too, had to be tried by a court of twenty-three judges.[9] Cases could not be tried on Friday, for if convicted, the condemned could not be executed on the following day; and to postpone the execution till Sunday was delay of justice (*einui din*)—probably causing the convicted unnecessary anguish.[10]

As with all capital punishment transgressions, those connected with the Sabbath, too, exempt one from financial liability incurred while transgressing. Thus, one who ignites a field or wounds a neighbor on the Sabbath does not have to compensate the injured because physical penalty (lashes, for igniting a fire, according to Rabbi Yose) or capital punishment is possible.[11]

2.

In the days of the Temple, commission of a Sabbath transgression subjected one to sin-offering (hatat). Since the sacrifice was the overt act of inner repentance, we find the interesting law that one who commits, in one span of forgetfulness, transgressions within all thirty-nine categories of work forbidden by the Torah, has to bring thirty-nine sacrifices.[12] According to the Mishna, one who forgets the *principle* of the Sabbath brings only one sacrifice for all the transgressions he commits during the Sabbaths of his forgetfulness. (His error is in forgetting the basic institution of the Sabbath, and for that he repents when he brings one sacrifice.) One who remembers the principle of the Sabbath, but forgets that *today* is Sabbath brings one offering for each Sabbath. (His error was not in thinking that the particular types of work are permissible, but in forgetting that the day was Sabbath, and therefore brings one sacrifice for the Sabbath. However, the days intervening between the Sabbaths during the span of his forgetfulness render each Sabbath a separate error.) One who remembers the principle of the Sabbath, and that today is Sabbath, but has forgotten which categories of work are forbidden, brings a sacrifice for each category of work, but only one for several acts within each category.[13] One brings an offering only for a transgression begun and concluded in error. Hence, one who reminded himself, after throwing an object, but before it landed, that it is forbidden to move an object four cubits in a public domain does not bring a sacrifice.[14]

A convert to Judaism who was never told about the Sabbath because of living among non-Jews, and a Jew taken captive as a child, bring only one sacrifice for all transgressions, for they commit only one error. According to Monobaz, they do not bring even one sacrifice, for theirs was not a case of error but of complete lack of knowledge.[15]

3.

Even during the days of the Temple, but especially after its destruction, religious leaders sought to discourage Sabbath desecration and to encourage its observance by pointing out punishments for desecration and rewards for observance. These concerned physical and spiritual well-being in this world, in the world-to-come and in the Messianic Age. Examples of the first are these teachings: "For three transgressions women die at childbirth—for negligence connected with the laws of *Nidah, Hallah* and lighting of (Sabbath) candles."[16] "He who keeps the Sabbath is kept far from sin."[17] Rabbi Eliezer ben Prata, commenting on the Torah verse ". . . to practice (literally, to do or to make) the Sabbath throughout their generations, an eternal covenant" (Exod. 31:16), declares, "He who keeps the Sabbath, is as if he created the Sabbath." Rabbi (Yehudah Hanassi) says, "He who keeps the Sabbath is as if he kept all the Sabbaths, from creation to the resurrection of the dead."[18] What the rabbis are saying, apparently, is that Sabbath observance makes one a creator of Judaism and a link in a chain of spiritual transmission, dating back to the beginning of time, and destined to go on to the end of time.

In the second group of promised rewards and punishments we find the following: The Torah says, "And keep

My statutes and laws, which if a man do, he shall live by them, I am the Lord" (Lev. 18:5). This, comments the *Sifra*, cannot refer to this world, for one must eventually die; but it must refer to the world-to-come.[19] The author of Jubilees is even more explicit. Although he decrees death even for desecrations forbidden only rabbinically, he threatens those who desecrate the Sabbath with eternal damnation as well, saying: "He who desecrates this day shall be killed, and all who do any work on it, shall die eternally. . . . And every man who will keep it, and rest on it from all his work, holy and blessed will he be all the days, like us (the angels.)"[20]

In the third group of promised rewards we have the following examples: Rabbi Levi said, If Israel kept the Sabbath properly, even once, Messiah would come, for the Sabbath is equivalent to all the *mitzvot*.[21] Rabbi Eliezer of Modin says, If you succeed in keeping the Sabbath, God will give you these portions: Eretz Israel, the world-to-come, (leadership by) the Kingdom of David, the priesthood (of Aaron) and the Levites. You will be saved from three evil occurrences: The Day of Gog (the terrible wars associated with the days of Gog and Magog), the pangs preceding the coming of the Messiah, and the great Judgment Day.[22]

CHAPTER X

Beneficiaries and Keepers of the Sabbath

*"For I the Lord sanctify you. . . ." The holiness of
the Sabbath is like the holiness of the world-to-come;
and thus it says, (Psalms 92) "A psalm, a song for the
Sabbath day," for a world which is all Sabbath.*
(*Mekhilta*, Shabbata, 1).

*"Do not count as others do, but count with reference
to the Sabbath"; that is, the first day of the week, the
second day, etc. . . . Sabbath.*
(*Mekhilta*, Bahodesh, 7).

SABBATH OBSERVANCE has three general aspects: 1)
physical rest and relaxation; 2) abstention from various kinds
of work and dispensable weekday routines; and 3) the enjoyment of physical, religious and intellectual well-being. A
Jew (including, of course, the convert) and his entire family
are involved in all three aspects, with men and women differing somewhat in areas of observance, and with lesser participation by children. The Torah commands that the blessing
of physical rest be extended to one's servants and animals.
(According to Beit Shammai even one's vessels have to rest
on the Sabbath.) Rabbinic law forbids a Jew to benefit from
work performed by a non-Jew in behalf of a Jew or by his
request, unless it is for a *mitzvah* which should not be postponed. Because the Sabbath is not merely a vacation from
work, but primarily a holy day dedicated to the Creator of
the universe, some rabbis looked askance at a heathen's

111

acceptance of the Sabbath as a *mere day of rest without accepting the spiritual implications* of the Sabbath.

That women are not exempt from any of the prohibitions imposed upon men, both by the Torah and the rabbis, is stated by Rabbi Yehudah ben Batira. With the verse, "Everyone shall be in awe of his father and mother, and My Sabbaths keep, I am the Lord" (Lev. 19:3) as his text, Rabbi Yehudah declares: In connection with the Sabbath, there is no distinction (in obligation to observe) between men and women.[1] The Schools of Ishmael and Hezekiah taught that according to the Torah women as well as men are subject to all the punishment or penalties (physical or financial) commanded by the Torah for transgressions and damages.[2]

Women are required not only to light candles and to participate in the enjoyment of the Sabbath, but they are also obligated to fulfil the *mitzvah* of *kiddush,* because all who are subject to 'keep' (the negative commands) are subject also to 'remember' (the positive commands).[3]

The *Mekhilta* interprets the Torah's phrase "your son and your daughter" as referring to minor children, for grown children are already included in the word "you."[4] However, as with all *mitzvot,* the obligation of children to observe the Sabbath is mainly educational, without the force of punishment or even of rabbinic censure, unless the parent benefits from the act of the child. Thus, the Talmud tells that once Rabbi P'dat advised Rabbi Itzhak bar Bisma, who had lost the keys to the synagogue in a public domain, to lead small children there, so that they could find and return them. The Gemara asks, how can this be reconciled with the Mishna's teaching that a father must stop his minor child from putting out a fire, for a father is obligated to have his child rest? Rabbi Yohanan explains that putting out a fire pleases the parent (and the child realizes it); but

Rabbi Itzhak did not tell the children that he had lost the keys.[5]

From the verse, ". . . to know that I the Lord sanctify you," the rabbis deduce that we need not enforce Sabbath observance upon those who lack understanding, such as the feebleminded and demented.[6]

The Torah's command that ". . . your male and female servants, and the son of your handmaid shall be allowed to rest" is interpreted by the rabbis to refer to uncircumcized slaves as well as to children of the covenant.[7] According to Rabbi Akiva, an uncircumcized slave (bought from a heathen) has to keep the Sabbath as a Jew keeps the festivals (with preparation of food, *okhel nefesh,* permitted). But according to Rabbi Shimeon his duties are no more than a Jew's on a weekday.[8]

In a former chapter we discussed the laws forbidding one to have his animal carry, or to wear anything which might be considered a burden. However, one need not stop his dog from carrying out his food to the street.[9] Animals may not be sold to heathens who will work with them on the Sabbath.[10]

Letters must not be given to a non-Jewish messenger on Friday, for it appears as if the Jew hires the non-Jew to work for him on the Sabbath, even if the payment is for a period of days.[11] According to Beit Shammai one must not sell or give anything to a non-Jew on Friday unless the recipient can reach his home before dark. Beit Hillel say he may, if the non-Jew leaves the house before dark.[12] However, where a Jew might be tempted to desecrate the Sabbath, the rabbis permitted him to have a non-Jew perform a service for him. Thus, a Jew who finds himself on the road Friday when it is about to get dark may give his purse to his non-Jewish companion, to carry it for him, because, said Rabbi Levi, the Children of Noah (non-Jews) were commanded to keep the Seven Precepts of Noah but not the Sabbath.[13]

A non-Jew who wants to extinguish a fire for a Jew (and only financial loss is involved) is neither urged to do it nor told to desist.[14]

A Jew may use the water drawn by a non-Jew for his own cattle, but not if the two are acquainted, for in the latter case the Jew habituates the non-Jew to draw more than he needs for his own cattle, in order to have enough for the Jew's. One may not use water drawn by another Jew even if it was drawn in error or under compulsion.[15]

CHAPTER XI

Jewish Attitude to the Sabbath

THE SABBATH, from its embryonic stage, possibly during the patriarchal or Egyptian periods, and more probably from its post-Exodus infancy, evolved through the centuries into a solidly established, hallowed, complex, national Jewish institution. By the time of Hillel and Shammai in the first century BCE, and more so by the time the Mishna was edited at the end of the second century, not only was the character of the Sabbath fairly well set, but its hold on the hearts of almost all Jews was demonstrated during periods of religious persecution as well as in relatively peaceful times. The Sabbath, the *Mekhilta* states, will never cease for Israel. For "you find that every *mitzvah* for which the Jews gave their lives is firmly entrenched in their hearts; and every *mitzvah* for which they did not give their lives still has no hold on them. Thus, Sabbath, circumcision, Torah study, and family purity (*taharat hamishpachah*) for which they gave their lives remained with them; but the Temple, civil laws, sabbatical and jubilee year laws for which they did not give their lives, did not survive with them."[1]

The rabbis believed that dedication to the Sabbath not only preserved the Sabbath for the Jewish people, but also preserved the Jewish people, as is implied in the following Midrash: When Haman drew lots, on the Sabbath day, to destroy the Jewish people, Israel's patron angel declared before God, " (You stated) 'It is a sign between Me and the

Children of Israel *forever*' (Exod. 31:13). If you seek to destroy them (the Jews), first nullify the Sabbath, and then You will be able to destroy them."[2]

Indications of general Jewish observance of the Sabbath during talmudic days are the following incidents and laws.

Hadrian asked Rabbi Yehoshua ben Hananiah, "Am I not greater than Moses, for he is dead and I am alive?" To disillusion the Roman, Rabbi Yehoshua suggested that he ban the making of fires. In the evening the rabbi showed Hadrian smoke coming out from one of the homes, which upon investigation was discovered to be that of one of Hadrian's ministers. Rabbi Yehoshua then pointed out that the ruler's decrees were being violated even during his lifetime, whereas Moses' were being kept even long after he died.[3]

Rabbi Hiya bar Abba visited Ludkia, where he was entertained most lavishly by his wealthy host. Asked why he merited such splendor, the host replied that in his former trade of butcher he always kept the best animals for the Sabbath.[14]

Until when may one return a deficient *sela*, the Mishna asks. It answers: In cities, until the recipient can show it to a money changer; and in villages, until the eve of the Sabbath. Rashi explains that in the villages, where there are no money changers, the *sela* is kept until Friday, when it is spent for Sabbath needs (and then the owner discovers whether or not his coin has full value).[5]

Rabbi Zakkai was asked, By what merit did you reach old age? He answered that it was because he observed *kiddush* at all times. Once, his mother sold her bonnet in order to provide wine for *kiddush*. (In the end, the story goes, they owned thousands of barrels of wine.)

Rabbi Huna wore a belt of reeds. Rav asked him where his good belt was, and he answered that he had pawned it in order to obtain money for *kiddush* wine. Rav blessed him that he should some day be able to afford silken garments.[6]

In time of a drought, Rabbi (Yehudah Hanassi) decreed a fast, without beneficial result. However, when Ilfa prayed, rain did come down. Rabbi asked him why he was able to achieve what Rabbi failed to effect. Ilfa explained that it was because he provided his poverty-stricken fellow-villagers with wine for *kiddush* and *havdalla*.[7]

Rabbi Hanina ben Dosa's daughter, looking sad one Sabbath eve, was asked by her father for the reason. She told him that in place of oil she had put vinegar in the lamp. He told her that it, too, could burn like oil; and, miraculously, it did, the entire Sabbath, and was even used for *havdalla*.[8]

Jewish loyalty to the Sabbath was characteristic of Jews in the Diaspora as well as in Palestine. In answer to Rabbi Ishmael bar Yose's question, By what merit do the Jews of the Diaspora enjoy life? Rabbi answered, By merit of their honoring the Sabbath and festivals.[9]

A famous story is told about a Jewish tailor in Rome, who always honored the Sabbath and festivals. One day, when fish was extremely scarce in the market place, he outbid a minister's servant, and bought the only available fish at a very exorbitant price. The minister asked why his fish course was absent and was informed about the incident. The minister then summoned the *hasid*, and accused him of having found a royal treasure, for otherwise how could he afford to pay such an exorbitant price? The tailor explained that he always bought fish in honor of his holy day, even at prices beyond his financial means. The minister accepted the explanation. (The pious man was rewarded by God, for he discovered a diamond in the fish, and the sale money sufficed for his lifetime needs.)[10]

2.

There were exceptions, however, to the general Jewish dedication to the Sabbath. Those who strayed from or neglected its observance were usually Jews who associated very closely with the heathens, or who lived in a heathen environment. What led Elisha ben Abuya (teacher of Rabbi Meir) to become an apostate (and to desecrate the Sabbath, openly), the Talmud Yerushalmi asks. In answer, it gives two interrelated causes. Elisha once saw a man climb a tree on a Sabbath, remove the mother bird from the nest (contrary to the command of Deuteronomy 22:6-7) and come down safely. But another man, who went up after the Sabbath, and who sent the mother away before he took her young (in accordance with the Torah command) was bitten by a snake. Elisha also read sectarian books and sang Greek songs,[11] and these, apparently, influenced him to turn from Judaism.

Types of Sabbath desecration mentioned in the Talmud as reasons for rabbinic restrictions or divine punishment suggest that the transgressors associated with the heathens and learned their ways. Tur Shimeon, state two rabbinic sources, was destroyed because its inhabitants played ball on the Sabbath.[12] Said Rabbah, people become poor because they survey their fields on the Sabbath (to ascertain needed repairs or improvements), and because they set their meal time for hour when the lecture in the synagogue is being delivered. Rabbi Hiyya bar Abba said, There were two families in Jerusalem who were destroyed, one because it set its Sabbath meal time at the time of the lecture, and the other because it set its meal just before the commencement of the Sabbath (and thus entered the Sabbath not craving food, as one is required to feel).[13]

Bar Kappara taught, First it was permitted to bathe in

warm water heated on Friday. When the bath houses started
heating on the Sabbath, claiming that it was done on Friday,
the rabbis forbade hot baths, but still permitted steam baths.
People then used to bathe, claiming that they only took steam
baths, and so the rabbis forbade steam baths, but still permitted hot springs. People then used to bathe in hot water,
claiming that they bathed in the warm waters of Tiberias,
and so the rabbis forbade the warm waters of Tiberias, but
permitted cold baths. Later the rabbis realized that this
could not stand (that is, the people would desecrate the
Sabbath, anyway) and so permitted, once again, the warm
waters of Tiberias.[14]

In Eretz Israel, a generally observant community, we find
this law, One who plants in error on the Sabbath need not
uproot it, because . . . said Rabbi Meir . . . Jews are prone
to be careless about the sabbatical year but not about the
Sabbath.[15] But a century later, in Babylonia, where some
communities were Judaically ignorant and negligent, Rav
stated, First the rabbis said that one who cooks on the Sabbath, in error, or who forgot the pot on the stove, Friday
at dusk, may eat the food. When those who pretended to
forget became numerous, the rabbis declared that even those
who really forget may not eat the food.[16]

Even Philo had to urge his fellow Alexandrian Jews not
to neglect the observance of the Sabbath, as the following
excerpt shows:

> But let us not for this reason (that the Sabbath is a
> reminder of God's power and of the limitation of the
> created beings) abrogate the laws laid down for its
> observance, and light fires or till the ground or carry
> loads or institute proceedings in court or act as jurors
> or demand the restoration of deposits or recover
> loans. . . . It is true also that the keeping of festivals
> is a symbol of gladness of soul and of thankfulness to

God. . . . We shall be ignoring the sanctity of the Temple and a thousand other things if we are going to pay heed to nothing except what is shown by the inner meaning of things. Nay, we should look on all outward observances as resembling the body, and their inner meaning as resembling the soul. It follows that exactly as we have to take thought of the body because it is the abode of the soul, so we must pay heed to the letter of the laws. If we keep and observe these, we shall gain a clearer conception of those things of which these are symbols; and besides that we shall not incur the censure against us.[17]

The rabbis sought to prevent possible Sabbath desecrations by discouraging unnecessary association with heathens, even in the endeavor to have the heathens adopt some basic Judaic practices such as rest on the Sabbath or study of the Torah. This, we believe, is the implied meaning of the rabbis in the following famous passage: ". . . 'for it is a sign between Me and you for your generations, to know that I, the Lord, sanctify you. Keep the Sabbath because it is holy to you' (Exod. 31:13-14) . . . to you, and not to the heathens (who have not accepted circumcision)." From this the sages inferred that heathens who keep the Sabbath will not only fail to receive reward, but will even merit death by Heaven. This is analogous to a king conversing with a noblewoman (matron). He who intrudes merits death."[18] (This was directed either at heathens who did not become full converts, or more likely at Jews who sought such partial conversions. See also, Note.)

The rabbis tried to encourage those who were forced to work for heathens, or who were captured by heathens (and by necessity lost memory of the Sabbath) to keep as much of it as possible, or at least to keep its memory alive. The verse, "My Sabbaths keep, and be in awe of My sanctuary, I am the Lord" (Lev. 19:30, 26:2) refers, say the rabbis, to

one who sells himself to a heathen. He must not say, Since
my master is an idolater, I too, shall be an idolater. . . . Since
he desecrates the Sabbath, I, too, shall desecrate it. Therefore, it says, "Do not make unto yourselves idols . . . My
Sabbaths keep. . . ." (Lev. 26:1-2). "I can be trusted to give
you reward" (for loyalty in difficult circumstances).[19]

Said Rabbi Huna, If one travels in a desert, and does
not know when Sabbath is, let him count six days and keep
the seventh. Hiyya bar Rav says, He keeps the first day and
works six days. Rabbi Huna reckons according to creation
(with the Sabbath being the seventh day). Hiyya figures
according to Adam (who rested the first day after he was
created). The lost man may take care of all of his needs on
the day that he designates as a sabbath, except that he should
begin the day with the *kiddush* and conclude it with the
havdalla (with the aim of not forgetting the real Sabbath).[20]

CHAPTER XII

Attitude of the World to the Sabbath

THE SABBATH according to Exodus, Ezekiel, Jubilees and the rabbis, was a reminder of the covenant between God and the Jewish people. The world, too, at least from the days of the Babylonian exile, regarded the Sabbath as a peculiarly Jewish institution. The non-Jewish reaction to the Sabbath varied with the centuries and groups, depending more on the cultural climate of the age and of a particular society than on a country. There were converts to the entire philosophy and way of life of the Sabbath. Others accepted only its idea but not its mode of observance, or its particular day. There were pagan rulers who respected the Jewish right to keep the Sabbath even to the extent of exempting the Sabbath adherents from military or official duties on the holy day. On the other hand, there were not only rulers who persecuted Sabbath observers but there were also pagan intellectuals who could not comprehend the view and way of the Sabbath, and therefore ridiculed it and its followers.

The Jews, in response either to cultural or social pressures, reacted in turn in their own way to the world's attitude or measures. At times, Jewish leaders encouraged non-Jewish acceptance of the Sabbath; and at other times, especially when the acceptance was only partial, discouraged it.[1] They defended, physically or politically or polemically, the Sabbath and their people's right to keep it. Unfortunately, there were also Jewish apostates, who not only abandoned their faith and their people, but also schemed to compel their former co-religionists to desecrate the Sabbath. Some of these apostates even came from illustrious social and academic homes.

It is interesting, and no doubt significant, that non-Jewish favorable response to the Sabbath occurred during, or prior to, Jewish political decline, when the Jewish people came in contact with other cultures. Thus, in the sixth century BCE, most likely in Babylonia (where Ezekiel not long before urged his fellow exiles to keep the Sabbath as a means of distinguishing and sanctifying themselves) deutero-Isaiah was declaring to prospective converts, ". . . Thus saith the Lord . . . to those of foreign descent, who attach themselves to God, to serve Him . . . everyone who keeps from desecrating the Sabbath, and keeps My covenant (probably circumcision), I will bring to My holy mountain, and cause him to rejoice in My house of prayer . . . for My house shall be called a house of prayer for all peoples" (Isaiah 56). Deutero-Isaiah was so impressed by the non-Jewish attitude to Judaism that he felt inspired to prophesy that eventually "every new moon and every Sabbath all flesh shall come to bow before Me, said the Lord" (ch. 66).

Six centuries later, Philo in Alexandria and Josephus in Rome described the respect with which Greeks, Romans and other pagans regarded the Sabbath. Philo writes:

We may fairly say that mankind, from East to West, every country and nation and state, show aversion to foreign institutions, and think that they will enhance the respect of their own by showing disrespect for those of other nations. It is not so with ours. They attest and win the attention of all, of barbarians, of Greeks, of dwellers on the mainland and islands . . . of the whole inhabited world, from end to end. For who has not shown this high respect for the sacred Seventh Day, by giving rest and relaxation from labor to himself and his neighbors, free-man and slaves alike, and beyond these to his beasts? For the holiday extends also to every herd . . . to every kind of tree and plant; for it is not permitted to cut any shoot or even a leaf, or to pluck any fruit whatsoever. All such are set at liberty on that day, and live as it were in freedom, under the general edict that proclaims that none touch them.[2]

Josephus, writing approximately five decades later, expresses ideas similar to Philo's. He states:

. . . Our laws have been such as have always inspired admiration and imitation among all other men. . . . The multitude of mankind have had a great inclination of a long time to follow our religious observances; for there is not any city of the Grecians nor of the barbarians, nor any nation whatsoever, whither our custom of resting on the Seventh Day has not come . . . and as God Himself provides all the world, so has our law passed through all the world, also.[3]

The friendly reaction to the Sabbath (and other aspects of Judaism) led to a counter reaction, first among the pagans, and later among Christian leaders. They sought to suppress the Sabbath, to exploit its observance by the Jews against them, and to ridicule or argue them out of adhering to it. In the second century BCE, the Syrian-Greeks used physical force to compel the Jews to abandon their faith, and apparently they also utilized scorn, as is implied in the following passage in II Maccabees:

Nicanor, hearing that Judas and his company were in strong positions about Samaria, decided to attack on the Sabbath day. The Jews who had been compelled to accompany him, said, "Give honor to the day which He, Who sees all things, has honored by sanctifying it

above all others." Nicanor demanded to know if there
is indeed a mighty One in heaven Who commanded the
Sabbath to be kept. The Jews answered, "There is in
heaven a living Lord, and a mighty One, Who commanded the Seventh Day to be kept." Nicanor answered,
"I also am mighty upon earth, and I command you to
take arms, and to do the king's business."[4]

Ridicule and scorn were used by the educated people as
well as by the masses during the Roman period. Thus,
"Seneca himself censures (the Sabbath) observers for the
ensuing loss of one-seventh of man's labor"[5] And Flaccus
Persius writes: ". . . and lamps holding violets, which are
placed at the greasy window discharge a heavy fume, and
the tail of tunny fish swims around in a red platter, and the
white bowl swells with wine, thou movest thy lips silently,
and fearest the circumcized Sabbaths."[6]

How the populace treated the Sabbath is described in
the Midrash. Taking as its text the verse in Psalms (69:13),
"They who sit at the gate discuss me the entire day," the
Midrash declares:

> These are the nations of the world who sit in the
> theaters and circuses, and discuss and ridicule me, after
> they have eaten and drunk. They exclaim (mockingly),
> "That we should not be in need of carob fruit like the
> Jews." They ask (mockingly), "How long do you want
> to live?"; and answer, "As long as the Sabbath garments
> of the Jews" (used only on the Sabbath, and hence last-
> ing long). They bring in a camel, with his wraps, and
> they ask, "For whom does he mourn?" They answer,
> "The Jews keep the sabbatical year, and not having
> vegetables, eat up his thorns." They bring in a clown,
> with shaven head, and ask (one another), "Why is this
> one's head shaven?" They answer, "The Jews keep the
> Sabbath, and whatever they earn during the week eat
> up on the Sabbath. Having no wood, they break and

use their beds for fuel. They have to sleep on the floor; and since they become covered with dust, they anoint themselves. Oil, therefore, becomes costly, and the clown, not being able to afford it, shaves off his hair."[7]

Physical and verbal attacks compelled the Jews to defend themselves physically (where possible), and politically. Thus, Josephus tells how Nicolaus pleaded the case of the Jews in Ionia by declaring, "The Seventh Day is a day of rest, dedicated to the study of laws, in order to avoid sin. An examination of the observance will reveal its intrinsic goodness and ancient date."[8] In the Talmud we are told that once (probably during the reign of Hadrian) Rome decreed that the Jews desecrate the Sabbath and leave their children uncircumcized. To thwart the decree, Reuben ben Astrobal cut his hair to appear like the Romans, and took a seat among them (that is, he, a "Romanized" Jew, used his position in behalf of his co-religionists). He said to the Roman officials, "Should one seek the impoverishment or enrichment of his enemies?" They answered, "Impoverishment." He continued, "Then let them (the Jews) rest on the Sabbath." They agreed, and revoked the decree.[9]

A different approach in dealing with an anti-Sabbath decree is related in other sources, in explanation why the twenty-eighth of Adar was proclaimed a day on which fasting was forbidden. The Roman government banned the study of Torah, circumcision and observance of the Sabbath. Judah ben Shamua and his colleagues went to a Roman noblewoman (matron) for advice. She advised them to cry out, in protest, at night. They heeded her advice, and protested. They cried out, "O heavens: Are we not your brothers? Are we not all sons of one father and of one mother? Why do you differentiate us from all other nations? Why do you decree against us these harsh laws?" (Apparently, they appealed, as loyal Roman citizens or subjects, to Rome's official tolerance for religious differences among her subjects.) The Roman government thereupon repealed the decrees; and that day, the twenty-eighth of Adar, was declared a holiday.[10]

2.

The appeal of the Jewish Sabbath (and other Judaic views and ways of life), the courage of the Jews in coping with persecution, and the dissemination of Judaic ideas, engendered an atmosphere conducive to the spread of Christianity. Its teachers, especially since Paul, stressed eschatology and creed, and hence sought to minimize the mother religion's emphasis on ritual and law. Later on (when they began to observe the first day of the week as the Sabbath) the Christians tried to negate the retention of the seventh day as the Sabbath. The Jews endeavored to defend both the day and the practical observance of the Sabbath. This we see reflected in the New Testament, in the writings of the church fathers, and in the talmudic literature.

The Paulist disparagement of Sabbath observance is seen in the following excerpts from the Gospels:

At that time Jesus went through the standing grain on the Sabbath; and his disciples, being hungry, began to pluck ears of grain and to eat. But the Pharisees, seeing it, said to him, "Thy disciples are doing what is not lawful for them to do on the Sabbath." But he said to them, "Have you not read what David did when he and those with him were hungry? How he entered the house of God, and ate shew bread which neither he nor those with him could lawfully eat, but only the priests? Or have you not read (sic:) that on the Sabbath days the priests in the Temple break the Sabbath and are guiltless? But I tell you that one greater than the Temple is here. But if you know what this means, "I desire mercy and not sacrifice," you would never have condemned the innocent, for the Son of Man is Lord even of the Sabbath.

And when he passed on from that place he entered their synagogue. And behold, a man with a withered hand was there. And they asked him, saying, "Is it lawful to cure on the Sabbath?" that they might accuse him. But he said to them, "What man is there among you who, if he has a single sheep and it falls into a pit on the Sabbath, will not take hold of it and lift it out. How much better is a man than a sheep: Therefore, it is lawful to do good on the Sabbath." Then he said to the man, "Stretch forth thy hand." And he stretched it forth, and it was restored, as sound as the other.[11]

But the ruler of the synagogue, indignant that Jesus had cured on the Sabbath, addressed the crowd, saying, "There are six days in which one ought to work; on these therefore come and be cured, and not on the Sabbath." But the Lord answered him and said, "Hypocrites: Does not each one of you on the Sabbath loose his ox or ass from the manger, and lead it forth to water? And this woman, daughter of Abraham as she is, whom Satan has bound, lo, for eighteen years, ought not she to have been loosed from this bond on the Sabbath?"

And as he said these things, all his adversaries were put to shame; and the entire crowd rejoiced at all the glorious things that were done by him.[12]

Now a certain man was there who had been thirty-eight years under his infirmity. When Jesus saw him lying there, and knew that he had been in this state for a long time, he said to him, "Dost thou not want to get well?" The sick man answered him, "Sir, I have no one to put me into the pool where the water is stirred; for while I am coming, another steps down before me." Jesus said to him, "Rise, take up thy pallet and walk." And at once the man was cured. And he took up his pallet and began to walk. Now that day was a Sabbath.

The Jews therefore said to him who had been healed, "It is the Sabbath; thou art not allowed to take up thy pallet." He answered them, "He who made me well said to me, 'Take up thy pallet and walk.'" They asked him, "Who is the man who said to thee, 'Take up thy pallet and walk'?" But the man who had been healed did not know who it was, for Jesus had slipped away, since there was a crowd in the place.

Afterwards Jesus found him in the Temple, and said to him, "Behold, thou art cured. Sin no more, lest something worse befall thee." The man went away and told the Jews that it was Jesus who had healed him.

And this is why the Jews kept persecuting Jesus, because he was doing these things on the Sabbath. Jesus, however, answered them, "My Father works even until now, and I work." This, then, is why the Jews were seeking the more to put him to death; because he was not only breaking the Sabbath, but he was also calling God his own Father, making himself equal to God.

In answer, therefore, Jesus said to them, "Amen, amen, I say to you, the Son can do nothing of himself, but only what he sees the Father doing. For whatever He does, this the Son also does in like manner."[13]

According to some authorities Christians began to observe Sunday as the Lord's day even before the destruction of the Second Temple.[14] Christian teachers sought to undermine the validity of Jewish insistence on the holiness of the seventh day and on the need to abstain from prohibition activities. This controversy we find reflected in various rabbinic sources, as in the following examples. Turnus Rufus asked Rabbi Akiva, "Why is this day more important than other days?" Rabbi Akiva answered, "Why is this man (Turnus Rufus) more important than other men?" Turnus Rufus answered, "The emperor so desires." Rabbi Akiva answered, "God also chose the Sabbath."[15]

Turnus Rufus asked Rabbi Akiva, "How do you know that the Sabbath is really the right day of rest?" Rabbi Akiva cited the rest of the River Sabbation and the rest of those condemned to hell.[16] Turnus Rufus continued, "If God really decreed the Sabbath, let Him not bring down rain and cause the grass to grow on the Sabbath." Rabbi Akiva answered, "In His own house God may move objects from room to room just as a Jew may carry within his private domain from place to place."[17]

Despite the attempts by their leaders to undermine the rabbinic Sabbath, there were Christians who found the Jewish Sabbath attractive. "In order to both impress the as yet unconverted masses of pagans and to fortify Christians, often still wavering, it became necessary to degrade the synagogue and its sister institutions. The frequent complaints of such church fathers as St. Chrysostom that Christians were attending synagogue services on Sabbaths and Jewish holidays, listening to Jewish sermons . . . furnished a realistic background to harsh discriminatory legislation."[18]

Meanwhile, Jewish teachers sought to fortify their own people, by pointing out the significance of the Sabbath for the Jewish people. They also tried to keep their followers from offending their neighbors. " 'For it is a sign between Me and you' (Exod. 31:13), but not between Me and the heathen nations,"[19] was taught, probably, mostly for inspirational purposes. Said Rabbi Yudon, " 'Remember' God gave to the nations of the world, and 'Keep' to Israel."[20]

NOTES

CHAPTER I

1. GENESIS RABBAH, 10:9
2. BABA BATRA, 120b
3. PESIKTA RABBATI, 23:9; GENESIS RABBAH, 11:7. However, in GENESIS RABBAH 64:4 it is stated that Abraham knew and kept the laws of the Sabbath, including those of the Oral Law.
4. NUMBERS RABBAH, 14:2
5. Moses verified his calculation when the *manna* did not come down on the Sabbath. Midrash, quoted in TORAH SH'LE-MAH, Exodus, p. 75, Note 93
6. EXODUS RABBAH, 1:28
7. Source given in Note 6
8. EXODUS RABBAH, 5:18
9. SHABBAT, 87b; YALKUT SHIMONI, *Beshalah*, 257. Nahmanides comments:

> "In Marah He gave them . . . the Sabbath," says Rashi; and this is the opinion of the rabbis. . . . The purpose was to habituate the people to the *mitzvot* and to ascertain whether they would accept (the Sabbath) willingly and joyously; and this is the test to which the Torah refers. . . . The plain meaning (however) is that when they came to the great, frightful and arid desert God gave them rules to follow, in order to enable them to survive until they entered inhabited land, for a rule *(minhag)* is also called *hok* and *mishpat* (the words used here by the Torah).

10. That day, according to the *Mekhilta,* was a Sabbath, which had been occurring regularly from the creation of the world until God commanded its observance on the twenty-second of the month, also a Sabbath, as was the day on which the Torah was given. MEKHILTA, *Vayassa,* 2; SHABBAT, 87b, 88b
11. In his anger, says the Midrash, Moses forgot to tell the Israelites that on the sixth day they should gather two

omers per person. Later, when they discovered that what they had gathered on Friday was double the usual amount, and the princes came and told Moses, he recalled God's command. Because Moses had forgotten to tell the Israelites, God included him when He rebuked them with the words, "Until when will *you* (including Moses) refuse to keep My commandments?" EXODUS RABBAH, 25:10

12. The *Mekhilta* magnifies the miracle of the double portion by stating that not only did the Israelites receive their *Sabbath's* supply on Friday, but they also received a double portion for the Sabbath. The double portion is referred to in the Torah by the words *lehem mishne,* which the *Mekhilta* amends to *lehem meshune,* a different portion, "that is, every day they gathered one omer, but for the Sabbath they gathered two omers; every day the *manna's* savor spread, but for the Sabbath even more; every day the *manna* shone like gold, but on the Sabbath even more." MEKHILTA, *Vayassa,* 3

13. MEKHILTA, *Bahodesh,* 7
    in his commentary on Exodus 20:8, Nahmanides explains the *Mekhilta* to mean that 'Remember' (*Zakhor*) was written on both Tablets, but that Moses put 'Observe' (*Shamor*) in Deuteronomy (his review of the Torah) in order to instruct the Israelites that God had also proclaimed 'Observe.'

14. PESIKTA RABBATI, 23:11 (See also *Sifra,* beginning of *Behukotei.*)

15. In his commentary on Ezekiel 20:12, Rabbi David Kimhi (the *RADAK*) says ". . . This is the sign: God hallowed the Israelites; He set them apart from the nations . . . and from idolatry; and He gave them the Torah . . . the Sabbaths . . . (and) the festivals are reminders of the Exodus (all referred to, by Ezekiel, as 'Sabbaths').

16. MEKHILTA, *Vayassa* 6; ERUVIN, 51a

17. SHABBAT, 96 b

18. SHABBAT, 73a
    The MEKHILTA (*Shabbata,* 2) states that these categories of work were taught by Moses orally. The Talmud (SHABBAT, 49b, 96b), however, infers the main classes of work from the kinds of work used in the construction of the Tabernacle. "For we have been taught, one is *hayav* only

for the kind of work present in the construction of the Tabernacle."

19. However, many of the acts necessarily connected with trading obviously belong in the categories forbidden by the Torah.

20. SIFREI, *Sh'lah L'kha;* BABA BATRA, 119a

21. Generally, in the Temple only public sacrifices were offered on the Sabbath. According to the rabbis, the Ephraimite prince's sacrifice was allowed to be brought on the Sabbath, even in the Tabernacle (which was of less durable holiness than that of the Temple), by special divine command. (MOED KATAN, 9a; NUMBERS RABBAH, 14:1.) According to the same Midrash, also by God's command, Joshua was permitted to wage war on the Sabbath. Because he conquered Jericho on the Sabbath, Joshua was requested to consign all the captured wealth to the treasure house of the Tabernacle. (See also JOSHUA, 6:15-24.)

22. SOFERIM, 10:1

23. BABA KAMA, 82a

CHAPTER II

1. Hutton Webster, ENCYCLOPEDIA OF RELIGION AND ETHICS, Vol. X, pp. 885-9.

2. The seven day week was probably adopted because of the seven planetary bodies, and the "period of lumination" can be roughly divided into four quarters of seven days each. (T. G. Pinches, *op. cit.,* pp. 889-91)

3. Prof. U. Cassuto, A COMMENTARY ON THE BOOK OF EXODUS (Hebrew), pp. 131-132

4. T. G. Pinches, *loc. cit.*

5. Prof. Bart, SEFER HASHABBAT, pp. 155-8

6. HOSEA, 2:13; AMOS, 8:5; II KINGS, 4:23; ISAIAH, 1:23; EZEKIEL, 45:17, 46:1

7. William R. Harper, A COMMENTARY ON AMOS AND HOSEA, p. 232

8. Solomon Goldman, THE BOOK OF HUMAN DESTINY, Vol. II, p. 744

9. Jacob Z. Lauterbach, RABBINIC ESSAYS, pp. 437-470

10. George Foote Moore, JUDAISM, Vol. II, p. 22

11. Prof. Bart, *op. cit.*

12. William F. Albright, THE ARCHAEOLOGY OF PALES-TINE, p. 236

13. I. Abrahams, ENCYCLOPEDIA OF RELIGION AND ETHICS, Vol. X, pp. 885-893

14. This accords with the rabbinic tradition that some of the Sabbath laws were given at Marah.

15. Dr. Albright and other great modern scholars regard the patriarchal stories as having a "historical nucleus through-out." Moses, according to Albright, most likely was familiar with the Egyptian and Canaanite cultures as well as with his native Hebrew and the Babylonian. (THE JEWS, HISTORY, CULTURE AND RELIGION, Dr. L. Finkel-stein, Ed., Vol. I, p. 3)

16. U. Cassuto, *op. cit.*

17. U. Cassuto, *ibid.,* p. 169.
   That Jewish institutions were not born in cultural vacuums, but in the context of their cultural environment, is implicit in the frequent biblical warning not to follow the ways of the Egyptians and Canaanites. That the influence was also positive, as suggested by Prof. Cassuto, can be inferred from a remarkable Midrash, which reads as follows: *"Anokhi* (meaning I, the first word of the Decalogue) is Egyptian. The Children of Israel learned to talk like the Egyptians, while they were slaves in Egypt. When God redeemed them, they could not understand Him. He said, 'I shall converse with them in Egyptian.' Therefore, He began with *Anokhi."* (TANHUMA, *Jethro*) The Midrash may be suggesting that the Israelites were able to grasp the new outlook because God related it to the ideas (or experiences) familiar to them.

18. This would bear out the rabbinic tradition that Jacob and Joseph observed the Sabbath.

19. The request may have been in the name of the religious heritage of the Israelites. Pharaoh was acquainted with the Israelite (Mesopotamian) tradition. Later on, when Moses demanded, in the name of Jehovah, "Let My people go," Pharaoh asked, "Who is Jehovah that I should listen to Him. . . . I do not know Jehovah" (Exod. 5:2) , thus imply-ing that he might have listened to a known god.

The Israelites probably used their day of rest to discuss their promised restoration to the land of the patriarchs.

20. A Midrash quoted by TORAH SH'LEMAH, (Vol. 8, p. 75) states that Moses thought back to creation and ascertained the right day for the Sabbath. This may mean that Moses arrived at a religious foundation for the Sabbath by reflecting upon the Babylonian cosmogony and arriving at the lofty outlook, the basis of the Sabbath, given in Genesis, and referred to in the Decalogue of Exodus.

21. EXODUS 3:12; 6:7; 7:16; 7:26, etc.

22. Jeremiah denounced carrying of burdens, specifically, because it was the enslaved poor who carried burdens for the rich. That this was the reason is seen from his promise of reward for observance of the Sabbath; that kings and servants will enter the same gates, and that the servants will not be compelled to carry their burdens through them on the Sabbath.

   Jeremiah and other prophets may have delivered a number of similar prophecies concerning the Sabbath, which were not recorded, because, in the words of the Talmud, "A prophecy needed for future generations was written down, but one not needed, was not written down." (MEGILLAH, 14a)

23. The Exodus 31:12-17 passage, giving the Sabbath as a sign of the covenant between God and Israel, reads as if written by a disciple of Ezekiel. (Unbiased scholars agree with Dr. William Albright that although much of the Pentateuchal material is even Mosaic in origin, the Pentateuch, in its present form, "was edited in approximately its present form during the Exile. There seems no adequate reason to deny that it was known in Jerusalem generations before Ezra, but it seems highly probable that it was Ezra who introduced the complete Pentateuch into normative Jewish use." (Albright, THE JEWS: THEIR HISTORY, CULTURE AND RELIGION, Vol. I, p. 54)

   A word as to why Ezekiel and Jeremiah emphasized different aspects of the Sabbath is in order. Jeremiah who foresaw Judah's collapse, and who linked cities with corruption and national decay, stressed the social aspects of the Sabbath. He glorified the Israelite sojourn in the desert, in his reaction against the evils of the city. He saw that the

136 A HISTORY OF THE SABBATH

Temple service did not transform the people of Judah, and so he minimized its importance. Ezekiel, on the other hand, having experienced the dangers of exile, the danger of total national disappearance, or extinction, stressed the Sabbath as a distinguishing force. Living in captivity, he felt that the Temple service could become a unifying and uplifting force, and therefore predicted its restoration, *per se*, as well as in connection with the Sabbath.

24. Salo Baron, A SOCIAL AND RELIGIOUS HISTORY OF THE JEWS, Vol. 1, p. 143
25. Baron, THE JEWISH COMMUNITY, Vol. 1, p. 63
26. Baron, HISTORY OF THE JEWS, Vol. 1, p. 145; R. Travers Herford, THE PHARISEES, p. 99
27. The distinctive role the Sabbath occupied in the Ezekiel era can be seen from a brief study of the meaning of the word 'sabbath.' The Alexandrian Jew-hater Apion identified the word sabbath with the word 'sabbao' a disease with which he claimed the Israelites were afflicted, and because of which they were expelled from Egypt. Apion added that because of this disease the Israelites had to rest after a six-day journey in the desert; hence, the seventh day became known as Sabbath. Josephus rightly ridiculed Apion's "explanation," and pointed to it as evidence of the author's impudence or ignorance (or vicious prevarication). Josephus explained that sabbath means 'complete rest.' (Josephus, AGAINST APION, Book 2, Section 2)

Marcus Jastrow associated the word sabbath with the Babylonian 'Shabbatu,' which originally meant the day of the full moon. (Cited in SABBATH, DAY OF DELIGHT, By Abraham E. Millgram, p. 339.) We are inclined to accept this explanation in a modified form. The word *shabbat,* related to the Babylonian *Shabbatu,* meant *a* day of complete rest (as explained by Josephus), and referred, in pre-Exilic days, to the Sabbath and the rest days of the festivals, but not to the new moon, which was a day of *partial* rest (as can be seen from a careful reading of chapter 20, verses 18-39, in I Samuel). Use of the word sabbath to mean the seventh day became customary only *after* Ezekiel.

An examination of the biblical use of the word *shabbat* and its derivatives will bear out our last statement. Genesis

2:1-3, referring to the seventh day, does not use the word *shabbat*, but only the words seventh day (three times), and the verbs *vayishbot* and *shavat* meaning, "He rested completely." In Exodus 16:25-30 the Torah again specifies the *seventh day*, and it uses the word *shabbat* as *a* day of complete rest, and not as *the* day. In verse 29, *hashabbat* refers to the Sabbath; however, its use as a synonym for the seventh day is preceded and followed by a four-time reference to the seventh day, so that the meaning of the word is actually the day of complete rest described in the entire passage.'

In Exodus 20:8-11, the Torah does not speak of 'the Sabbath' but of 'the day of the Sabbath' (the day of complete rest) and of 'the seventh day.' Exodus 23:12 and 35:2-3; Leviticus 23:3; Numbers 29:9-10 and Deuteronomy 5:12-16 all use 'seventh day' and 'day of the Sabbath.' Exodus 31:12-17 uses 'seventh day' and *ha-shabbat* interchangeably because, as pointed out earlier, that passage was composed by a disciple of Ezekiel, under whose influence *Shabbat* began to mean the seventh day.

Our approach that *shabbat* originally meant a day of complete rest, and not necessarily the seventh day, is borne out by the rabbinic interpretation of *hashabbat* in Leviticus 23:15 as the first day of Passover, or the first day of complete rest. (MENAHOT, 66a). It also accords with the Torah's use of *shabbat* and *shabbaton* when speaking of the days of rest of the festivals. According to this, II Kings 4:23, Isaiah 1:13, Hosea 2:13, and Amos 8:5 refer to the days of complete rest of the festivals (whereas *hag* refers to the entire festival) as well as to the Sabbath. Verse 14 in Isaiah 1 "your new moons and festivals" would now correspond to verse 13 which would be translated "your new moons and rest days."

We mentioned that the verses 12-17 in Exodus 31 were written under the influence of Ezekiel. Some proof that the Torah was edited after the fall of the First Commonwealth is contained in the fact that while the Torah requires sacrifices on the new moon, the day is no longer treated as one of even partial rest, as it appeared to have been at the time of the authors of Kings, Isaiah, Hosea, Amos and especially Samuel. This was already noted by Rabbi Obadiah Sforno, who in his comment on Numbers 28:11 states: "The day of *Rosh Hodesh* used to be holy in Israel, in some way, as is said in Samuel 20, 'Where were you on the day of work?' —implying that the new moon was to them a day of rest."

See also Y. Kaufman, TOLDOT HA-EMUNAH HA-YISRAELIT, Vol. 1, p. 212, and Vol. 4, pp. 342-43

A possible valid reason for the abandonment of the new moon as a day of rest is suggested by Wellhausen, when he writes: "It may have been with a deliberate intention that the new moon was thrust aside on account of all sorts of heathenish superstitions which readily associated themselves with it." (Julius Wellhausen, PROLEGOMENA TO THE HISTORY OF ANCIENT ISRAEL, Meridian Library, pp. 112-113)

28. TOSEPHTA, *Shabbat,* 15:1
29. SHABBAT, 123b
30. Herford, THE PHARISEES, p. 60
31. *ibid.,* p. 66

That Judaism was not a gift presented in a "closed revelation," but the organic product of an "open," continuous revelation is implied by the rabbis themselves. The Talmud Yerushalmi states that Moses received on Mount Sinai even the future innovations of every senior or mature student (*talmid vatik*). (HAGGIGA 1:1; MEGILLAH 4:1) Isaac Hirsh Weiss, in his DOR, DOR V'DORSHOV (vol. 2, p. 2) interprets the statement to mean that even the future insights of students are already implicit in the Torah. That this interpretation is valid is seen from the famous talmudic legend, according to which God showed Moses Akiva building mounds and mounds of laws (*teilin, teilin shel halakhot*) on every point or stroke of the letters of the Torah. Moses was unable to comprehend the teachings, and he felt downhearted. However, when one of Rabbi Akiva's students asked, "Rabbi, how do you know this?" and Rabbi Akiva answered, "It is a Mosaic law from Mount Sinai" (*halakha l'Moshe miSinai*), Moses was reassured. (MENAHOT 29b) This legend implies that the seeds of later development of Judaism were inherent in early Judaic law, although the fruit was, outwardly, quite different from the roots.

The growth was in response to a new situation not

specified or included in the original legislation. The situation was met either by new legislation or by interpretation, or by a popular response (which after it became a custom was sanctified into law), all in the spirit of the related legislation, or for the greater benefit of Judaism. Examples of the first we find in the Torah itself. Moses had to consult God concerning the unclean people who could not observe the Passover in its due time (Numbers 9:6-14), the wood gatherer (Numbers 15:32-36) and the inheritance by the daughters of Zelophead (Numbers 27:1-11).

The use of interpretation (as pointed out by Weiss in his magnum opus, vol. 1, p. 8) co-existed with the written law. Thus, the Torah defines only a few of the kinds of work forbidden on the Sabbath. But that other kinds of work, too, were understood to be forbidden is obvious from the fact that the wood gatherer was brought before Moses and Aaron (to ascertain the *kind* of punishment, for the witnesses seemed to know that he deserved punishment), and from the fact that only on the festivals was the preparation of food (*okhel nefesh*) permitted. (According to the *baraita* in *Beitza*, 28b, work forbidden on the Sabbath is forbidden also on the festivals, except that which is necessary in the preparation of food.)

How early legislation was restored through interpretation by those with deep insight and dedication is exemplified in the dispute between Rabbi Akiva and Rabbi Tarphon (Triphon) as to whether handicapped priests (*baalei mumin*) sounded the *shofar* during the offering of a sacrifice. Rabbi Tarphon swore that he saw his maternal uncle, who was lame, sound the *shofar*. Rabbi Akiva answered, "Perhaps it was for *hakhel* (the gathering at Succot, every seventh year, for the reading of the Torah) and on Yom Kippur during the Jubilee year." Rabbi Tarphon recalled the incident, and admitted his error. "You are right," he exclaimed. ". . . Tarphon saw and forgot, but Akiva ascertains the *halakhah* by means of interpretation: He who departs from you, departs from life." SIFREI, *Beha'alotkha;* TALMUD YERUSHALMI, *Yoma,* 1:1

There were cases of laws, whose original rationale were forgotten, which continued in effect because of their sancti-

fication through time. Weiss thinks that the talmudic concept *halakhah l'Moshe miSinai* applies to such laws. (Weiss,
DOR, DOR V'DORSHOV, vol 2, pp. 195-196)

Some support for his view can be found in the following statement by Rabbi Yohanan: "If you come across a
law whose reason you no longer know, do not shove it aside,
for many laws were taught to Moses on Mount Sinai, and
all are embedded (*m'shukaot*) in the Mishna." (TALMUD
YERUSHALMI, *Peah*, 2:4)

Our rabbis believed that the meeting of new situations
with adequate interpretation or legislation in the tradition
of, and for the benefit of, Judaism saved it from becoming
stagnant and neglected. This belief is implicit in their declaration, "If Shaphan (the scribe who received the Book
of the Torah discovered in the days of Yoshiyahu, according to II Kings, ch. 22), Ezra and Rabbi Akiva had not
arisen, the Torah would have become forgotten from
Israel." (SIFREI, *Ekev*)

32. Herford, THE PHARISEES, p. 112
33. *ibid.,* p.121
34. Josephus, writing about four centuries later, remarks:
"Those who view this without prejudice, will see it is
praiseworthy when people regard their laws and fear of God
more precious than their freedom and freedom of their
country." (CONTRA APION, 1:22)

Rabbinic "hedges" were intended only to safeguard the
Torah from likely transgression. On the other hand, the
rabbis allowed their insight into the intent of the laws to
interpret the laws so as to ease possible rigors (as followed
by literalistic non-Pharisees). Thus, the Mishna declares:
"The laws of the Sabbath . . . are like mountains suspended
by a hair, with little scripture and many *halakhot,* without
much to lean on . . . but they are organic parts of the
Torah." (HAGIGAH, 10a) The Mishna, obviously, does not
refer to Sabbath restrictions, for it would not seek to undermine the validity of the restrictions, as such a statement
would tend to do, if it really applied to them. The Gemara,
therefore, explains that the Mishna refers to the principle
that the Torah forbids only intended work (*melekhet mahashevet*), although the Torah forbids all work. That the

Torah means to forbid only intended work, the rabbis
deduced from the construction of the Tabernacle—from
which the concept of Sabbath work is derived—where the
Torah speaks of *melekhet mahashevet*. Thus, without much
scriptural support, the rabbis freed would-be transgressors
from being regarded as breakers of Torah law, in the
various categories of Sabbath work.

35. I MACCABEES, 2
36. Josephus, THE WARS, BOOK I, 7:3
37. It is difficult to ascertain the exact dates of BOOK OF
    JUBILEES and FRAGMENTS OF A ZADOKITE WORK,
    but whether we place them earlier or later than the Macca-
    bean period they contain regulations prevalent among the
    Hassidim before the Maccabean revolt. Dr. Meyer Waxman
    points out that the Talmud, too, mentions that the death
    penalty was once given to one who rode on the Sabbath.
    It was a time of religious persecution, when there was danger
    that the transgressor's example would undermine the spirit
    of resistance.
         Dr. Waxman adds that not all rabbis agreed on the per-
    missibility of cohabitation on the Sabbath. Some Hassidim
    believed that pregnancy lasts 271-273 days. In order to pre-
    vent the possible desecration of the Sabbath, in case the
    birth should occur on a Sabbath, these Hassidim abstained
    from the Sabbath to Wednesday. Also, the permissibility of
    waging war on the Sabbath was still disputed in the days
    of Shammai. (Meyer Waxman, GALUT U'GEULAH
    B'SIFRUT ISRAEL, P. 156; SANHEDRIN, 46a)
38. A. M. Haberman, EDAH V'EDUT, pp. 113-115
39. Simon Dubnow, DIVRE YEME AM OLAM, Vol. II, pp.
    82-83, 182-183
40. Although the members of the School of Shammai were re-
    garded of keener intellect, the School of Hillel generally
    received the majority vote, because they were humble and
    congenial, and the *bat kol*—a heavenly echo, or the intui-
    tion of the people—favored their views. Even some students
    of Shammai, such as the pious Rabbi Yohanan of Horan,
    followed, in practice, Hillel's decisions.
         On rare occasions, due to the pressure of a situation and
    of Shammai's disciples, the majority accepted the Shammai-

ite views. Thus, when the Eighteen Decrees pertaining to
the Sabbath were adopted, Beit Shammai gained the majority decision. However, the followers of the two Schools
evaluated the results of the day, very differently. It was said
that "that day was as hard as the day when the Israelites
made the golden calf." Rabbi Eliezer, a follower of Shammai, said, "They filled the measure," that is, they established hedges in good measure. Rabbi Yehoshua, a disciple
of Hillel, declared, "They erased the measure," i.e., they
decreed more than the people could bear, and this led to
transgression. "It is comparable," said Rabbi Eliezer, "to a
barrel filled with nuts; the more poppy seeds one places
within, the better." "No," answered Rabbi Yehoshua, rather
"it is comparable to a barrel filled with oil; if one pours
water into it, the oil is forced out." (Talmud Yerushalmi,
SHABBAT, 1:4; Talmud Bavli, ERUVIN, 6b, 13b; YEVA-
MOT, 14a)

The law was decided by majority vote; why, then was
the minority vote also recorded? The Mishna asks this question, and answers: so that the opinion be available to future
courts; for possible reconsideration, according to one interpretation. But according to Rabbi Yehudah as interpreted
by Maimonides, it was recorded to prevent any future judge
from seeking the acceptance of the rejected view. (EDUYOT,
1:6)

41. EDUYOT, 5:6-7
42. ROSH HASHANAH, 14b
43. SHABBAT, 130a
44. YEVAMOT, 14a
45. SHABBAT, 130b
46. *Ibid.,* 37b
47. Rashi explains that the people, the *amei ha-aretz,* do not
    know that certain things may not be handled on the Sab-
    bath, but they side with the Pharisees, and want their view
    to prevail. (SUCCAH, 43b)
48. Talmud Yerushalmi, quoted by Rabbi Hananel, in SUC-
    CAH, 44a. Yerushalmi, SUCCAH, 4:1. Dr. A. Goldberg
    rightly pointed out to me that Rabbi Shimeon's instructions
    to the calendar formulators were issued in a period after
    the destruction of the Temple. Yet, it is true that Pharisees

were more tolerant of major differences of opinion within their own ranks than of lesser disagreements with the Sadducees.

49. The Sabbath, like all of Judaism, was from its very inception, for the benefit of man, for the preservation and enhancement of his life. Since the individual finds expression through the group, it was felt necessary to maintain the continuity of community worship and religious institutions, even if certain individual priests and their assistants, etc., had to desecrate the Sabbath in the process.

50. ROSH HASHANAH, 21b, 23b; ERUVIN, 45a

51. *Op. cit.*, 29b

52. Commenting on the verse, "And Moses said, Eat it *today*" (Exod. 16:25), Ibn Ezra writes:

> Many non-believers erroneously infer from this verse that the Sabbath should be observed beginning with the day . . . and speaking on the sixth day Moses said, *tomorrow* (implying that the Sabbath began *after* the night). They also interpret the verse, "And it was evening and it was morning one day" to mean that the first day was completed at *dawn* of the second. But (they) are mistaken, for Moses directed himself only to the custom of the Israelites . . . to do work during the day; therefore, he said, *tomorrow*. . . . The Torah says, "Seven days you shall eat matzos" which, the Torah says, begin at evening and end at evening. The Torah also says "From *evening* to *evening* rest on your sabbath." Also, if one met with an accident of uncleanliness, during the day or night, he became unclean until the *setting of the sun* (Deut. 23:11-12); and if it were so (that the day ended at dawn) then the Torah should have required the unclean man to bathe at dawn.

Other traditionalist commentators agreed with Ibn Ezra. Thus, Rabbi David Kimhi (*RaDaK*) explains that "It was evening and it was morning" really means, "It was night and it was day." The Torah, he explains, uses the word *boker* for the period from sunrise to sunset, to distinguish it from *yom*, which the Torah uses for the twenty-four hour span. Nahmanides, another great medieval biblical commentator, wrote in his comment on verse 1:4 of Genesis that "God created light but did not spread it out over the foundations until after a night's duration. Consequently, the night preceded the day." The traditionalist viewpoint was summed up by the compiler of the *Midrash Hagadol*, who says, "And it was evening and it was morning . . . tells us that darkness preceded light in creation; 'one day,' that is, the day follows the night; and you find everywhere that the night precedes the day." (MIDRASH HAGADOL, *Genesis*) This is an extension of the Mishna referred to in the next footnote.

53. HULIN, 83a; Lev., 23:28-30; See also BERAKHOT, 2a, b
54. NEDARIM, 76b
55. Jacob Z. Lauterbach, RABBINIC ESSAYS, pp. 437-470; TOSEPHTA, *Taanit*, 2:7
56. As proof that the Sabbath began at dawn he cites the following biblical references, where the word 'day' precedes the word 'night': Gen. 4:4, 8:22, 49:27; Exod. 13:21, 34:28; Lev. 8:35; Josh. 1:8; I Kings 8:59; Jeremiah 33:20; Jonah 2:1. In Deut. 28:66 and Jer. 14:17 the word 'night' precedes 'day,' but Dr. Zeitlin suggests that the Septuagint version, in which the sequence is reversed, is correct.
57. JEWISH QUARTERLY REVIEW, April 1946, pp. 403-414; Jan., 1954, pp. 183-193.

    As proof that the Sabbath began at sunset after the Restoration, Zeitlin cites the Book of Judith, where the heroine speaks of serving God night and day (11:17), and Tannaitic literature, where night precedes day. But, Dr. Zeitlin adds, "we must make it clear, however, that in the Temple the day was not reckoned according to the calendar. The Temple was opened during the day, and closed during the night . . . from sunrise to sunset."

    In *Fragments of a Zadokite Work*, probably corresponding in time to early Tannaitic literature (although not according to Dr. Zeitlin) we find this rule, shedding light on our question: "No man shall work on the sixth day from the time when the sun's orb in its fullness is still without the gate." (Ch. 13, R. H. Charles, translator)

    In partial support of Dr. Zeitlin's view one could cite the belief of some traditionalist scholars that until the Revelation on Mount Sinai the day preceded the night. (See article by Rabbi M. M. Kasher, in the *Genesis* volume of the MIKRAOT GEDOLOT.)
58. Cassuto, M'ADAM AD NOAH, pp. 15-17. The author accepts Rabbi Samuel ben Meir's (*RaShBaM*) interpreta-

tion of "And it was morning and it was evening" to mean that the day ended at dawn. It was against Rabbi Samuel that Ibn Ezra directed his acrid comments, from which we quoted above.

It seems to us that the worthy scholars who interpret *boker* in verse 5, 8, etc. of Gen. 1 to mean the 'dawn' err. For if that were the meaning, then verse 5 should read, "It was evening, and it was the dawn of the second day"; and verse 8 should read, "It was evening, and it was the dawn of the third day" (instead of, as it reads now, "of the first day; of the second day"; etc.); and verse 31 should read, "It was evening and it was the dawn of the *seventh* day" (instead of the sixth day). The real meaning of *boker* in ch. 1 of Genesis, as pointed out by the *RaDaK*, is daylight span, as distinguished from *yom*, which in this chapter refers to a 24-hour span. Of course *yom* has other meanings elsewhere, as pointed out by Ibn Ezra in his lengthy comment on Exod. 16:25.

59. It is worth noting that John (20:1), unlike Matthew, says, "Now on the first day of the week, Mary Magdalene came early to the tomb, while it was still dark. . . ."
60. Even if this chapter were the final product of a post-Exilic editor, the evening and morning sequence would indicate that at least in his day the Sabbath began at sunset.
61. As a folk tale of very early Israelite history, it, no doubt, records the day as it was then reckoned. That the story was not subject to later religious editing is evident from the fact that Samson's marrying of a heathen Philistine woman was not deleted or explained away.
62. Esther, of course, offers proof no more valid than any found in the Apocryphal books, for it may have been written during the Greek domination of Palestine.

Deuteronomy 5:7, "when you lie down and when you rise up," suggests that evening precedes morning. Also the psalmist (Psalms, 55:18) speaks of praying to God "evening, morning and noon."

CHAPTER III

1. Why was the *seventh* day chosen as the day of the Sabbath? As pointed out in Note 2 of Ch. II, the seven day week

was probably adopted because the "period of lumination,"
or the lunar month, can be divided into four quarters of
approximately seven days each; and this would make the
seventh day as the preferable day of rest. However, other
answers were given, some pointing to its mystical significance, and others to its choice by God. Thus, Ben Sira
writes:

> . . . The scornful man mocks everything. Why is this day different
> from all days, he says; do not all receive their light from the sun?
> But God in His wisdom distinguished them as festivals and yearly
> cycles. Some He chose to sanctify; and some He made ordinary
> days. Are not all mortal creatures made from clay, and man, too,
> was fashioned from earth? And yet in His wisdom, God divided
> them, and distinguished their ways. Some of them He blessed, and
> sanctified, and exalted to serve Him; and some of them He cursed,
> and brought low, and made an object of reproach. As clay in
> the potter's hand, to fashion it at his pleasure, so man is in the
> hand of his Maker; to every man He apportioned according to His
> will. (Ecclesiasticus 33:6-13).

An answer similar to Ben Sira's was given by Rabbi
Akiva. Asked by a Roman patrician why the Sabbath was
more important than other days, Akiva answered: "Why is
this man (the questioner) more important than other men?"
The Roman answered, "Because my lord (the emperor)
willed it." Rabbi Akiva was then able to make his point.
"So it is with the Sabbath, too," he said. "The Lord willed
it." (Sanhedrin, 65b)

"The reason for the creation of the world in six days,"
wrote Aristobulos, "is that the number seven has a great
mysterious importance in the creation and guidance of the
world." And Philo wrote, "The supremacy of the harmonious
number seven is pointed out by the mathematicians."
(SEFER HASHABBAT, pp. 14-15) It has also been suggested that it is the only integer between 1 and 10 that
can be neither dividend nor divider for any other number,
larger than 1, in that basic group.

The Midrash, commenting on the verse, "No dough shall
be seen in your possession for seven days" (Exod. 12:19),
says, "As there were seven days between the redemption and
the cleaving of the Red Sea, as creation was in seven days,

and as the Sabbath is once in seven days, likewise, shall these seven days be observed every year." (EXODUS RAB-BAH, 19:7)

A modern writer points to the popularity of the number seven in ancient times by listing the numerous times the number occurs in the Bible:

> Seven . . . has always been regarded as sacred and mystic. . . . There are seven days of creation; after seven days respite the flood came; the years of famine and plenty are in cycles of seven; every seventh day was a Sabbath; every seventh year, the sabbatical year; the feast of unleavened bread and the feast of tabernacles were observed seven days; the golden candlesticks had seven branches; seven priests with seven trumpets encompassed Jericho once a day, and seven times on the seventh day; Jacob obtained his wives by servitude of seven years; Samson kept his nuptials seven days, and on the seventh he put a riddle to his wife, and he was bound with seven withes, and seven locks of his hair were shaved off; Nebuchadnezzar was seven years a beast; Shadrach and his two companions in misfortune were cast into a furnace heated seven times more than it was wont.

(William S. Walsh, HANDBOOK OF LITERARY CURIOSITIES, quoted in Solomon Goldman's *Book of Human Destiny*, vol. I, pp. 296-297. See also S. L. Gordon's Hebrew Commentary on Deuteronomy 5:14.)

2. AVOT D' RABBI NATHAN, 11:1
3. MEKHILTA, *Bahodesh* 7; PESIKTA, 23:5; MIDRASH HAGADOL, *Genesis*, 2:2.

The same idea was expressed by the Greek-Jewish philosopher Aristobulos, and is implicit in a famous talmudic legend. Aristobulos wrote: "The Torah's statement that God rested on the seventh day does not mean to imply that He needed to rest. It means that God created the world according to definite laws, and He supervises their creation." (SEFER HASHABBAT, p. 14) In the talmudic legend, told by Rabbi Yehoshua ben Levi, the angels requested God to give them the Torah, and not to man, whom they regarded unworthy. Moses himself was at first confounded by their apparently justified request. However, with God's encouragement, Moses pointed out that the Torah is for those who have a need for it. "Do you work, that you need a day of rest?" Moses asked; and the angels approved the implied answer.

Rest, as a pre-condition for future creativity may also be implied in Gen. 2:3, in what at first sight appears as a redundant phrase, reading "And He rested from all His work, . . . which God created to do" (*asher bara Elohim la'asot*). It may mean that the rest was a prerequisite for continued creation. The idea of creation is expressed by the word *bara*, and the actual fulfilment by the word *la'asot*.

4. This is implied in the talmudic legend cited in the preceding note. The Talmud, following the *Mekhilta*, states, "It (the Sabbath) was handed over to you, and not you into its hands." (YOMA, 85b; MEKHILTA, *Ki Tisa*)

5. TOSEPHTA, *Berakhot*, ch. 3

6. MEKHILTA, *Shabbata*, 1

A modern biblical scholar inferred this idea from first three verses of Genesis 2. He writes: "The writer's (of the passage) idea of the Sabbath and its sanctity is that it is not an institution which exists or ceases with observance by man; the divine rest is a fact as much as the divine working . . . it is an ordinance of the cosmos like any other part of the creative operations, and it is for the good of man in precisely the same sense as the whole creation is subservient to his welfare." (John Skinner, A COMMENTARY ON GENESIS, p. 35)

7. EXODUS RABBAH, 19:7

Nahmanides, commenting on Deut. 5:12, writes: "Maimonides in the GUIDE stated that the first Decalogue (in Exodus) gives the reason for the establishment of the Sabbath. Here, however, the Torah warns us to keep the Sabbath because we were slaves and had no rest; now we should rest, and recall God's kindness to us. The second reason is not apparent from the observance of the Sabbath, but, rather, recalling the Exodus leads us to the awareness of God's guidance of the world." A similar interpretation is given by the commentator, OR HAYYIM.

The reference to Egyptian and Exodus experiences as evidence of God's providence may also be what the rabbis meant when they interpreted, "Therefore God blessed the day of the Sabbath" as a blessing with *manna*, for *manna* was the "bread from heaven" of the Israelites during their sojourn in the desert, and it was evidence of God's guidance and protection. It is significant that the Torah describes in comparative detail the close and miraculous relationship between the *manna* and the Sabbath. Other rabbis stated that the observance of the Sabbath was first commanded at Marah, where the Israelites first discovered water in the desert, for water, too, was a symbol of Israelite survival in the desert, and therefore of God's guidance and protection. (MEKHILTA, *Bahodesh*, 7; see note 10 in ch. I)

8. *Ibid.*, 8
9. *Op. cit., Shabbata*, 1.

Maimonides emphasizes that the Sabbath points to God's creation of the world out of nothing, which is designated as *hiddush ha-olam*, that is, renewal of the world. (GUIDE FOR THE PERPLEXED, II, ch. 31)

Rabbi David Kimhi says: "The Sabbath is a witness and a reminder that God created the world. . . . Therefore, the Sabbath was given before the Torah, for first had to come the knowledge of God as Creator and Lord." (Commentary, Isaiah, 56:6)

Nahmanides writes: "God . . . commanded us to make a sign and reminder that He created all. This reminder is the Sabbath. . . . Therefore, the rabbis said that the Sabbath is equivalent to all *mitzvot*, as they stated regarding the rejection of idolatry, for by keeping the Sabbath we testify to the fundamentals of our faith, namely creation out of nothing, providence and prophecy." (Commentary, Exodus, 20:8)

The conception of the Sabbath as a reminder of God's creation and Israel's sanctification may explain a remarkable Midrash, sometimes misinterpreted even by friends of Judaism. The Midrash states: "Heathens who keep the Sabbath not only will not receive reward, but even merit death. 'For it is a sign between Me and you.' (Exod. 31:13) This is analogous to a king and a noblewoman engaged in a dialogue. He who intrudes merits death." (EXODUS RABBAH, 25:11) The Midrash is telling us that the Sabbath is a reminder that God created the world. To remain an idolater while keeping the Sabbath is to commit idolatry

despite one's awareness of a supreme Creator. (It is also possible that the rabbis tried to urge Jewish sectarians, who continued to observe the Sabbath, to return to monotheism.) Of course, the statement "merits death" is not to be taken literally, but in the sense that the Mishna in *Avot* says that he who interrupts his study even to admire God's works merits death (AVOT, 3:9); and in the sense that the Talmud says that a scholar merits death if there is a grease spot on his garments. (SHABBAT, 114a)
10. Nathan Barack, FAITH FOR FALLIBLES, p. 25
11. SHABBAT, 119a
12. *Ibid.*, p. 119b

CHAPTER IV

1. SHABBAT, 96b
    The Talmud deduces it also from the verses, "Moses commanded, and a proclamation was issued throughout the camp, 'Let no one do any more work;' and the people stopped bringing." (Exod. 36:5-6) TOSAFOT, following ERUVIN (17b) infers it from the verse "Let no one go out from his place. . . ." (Exod. 16:29) by interpreting it to mean, "Let no one go out with his container to gather *manna*." SHABBAT, 2a. The ban on carrying four cubits in a public domain is a law taught by teacher to student (since Moses). SHABBAT, 96b
2. A type of work is regarded as only an offspring (*toldah*) or derivative of the parent or main category. Generally, similarity of purpose and performance determine whether an act belongs in one category or another. BABA KAMA, 2a; TIFERET YISRAEL, Introduction to Commentary on Mishna of SHABBAT
3. SHABBAT, 49b; TALMUD YERUSHALMI, *Shabbat,* 7:2
4. SHABBAT, 73a
    The Talmud refers to Jeremiah's denunciation of carrying on the Sabbath, although it is listed in the Mishna as one of the thirty-nine categories of work (present in the construction of the Tabernacle.) The additional source defining it as work, Tosaphot explains, is necessary because it is not easily recognized as work (*m'lakha g'rua*) since it does not involve any change in itself. (HORAYOT, 4a;

TALMUD YERUSHALMI, *Shabbat*, 1:1; TOSAFOT, *Shabbat*, 96b)

Dr. Y. M. Gutman groups the thirty-nine categories of work into broad divisions: agricultural, food preparation and handicrafts. The Torah indicates the first when it states, ". . . in plowing and reaping you shall rest" (Exod. 34:21). Related to plowing and reaping are such tasks as sowing, threshing, sifting, etc. Work involved in food preparation is indicated when the Torah states (Exod. 16:23), ". . . on the sixth day, they shall prepare that which they brought in; that which you wish to bake, bake, and that which you wish to cook, cook, and that which is left over, keep for tomorrow." In Numbers (11:8), the Torah tells us that the Israelites ground the *manna* in a mill or crushed it in a pestle or cooked it in a pot, and made it into cakes. All this was necessarily prepared on Friday. Within the second division of food preparation are grinding, kneading, baking, etc. The third division, comprising tasks performed by craftsmen, is implied in the Torah's law prohibiting Sabbath work, which is placed before the command to construct the Tabernacle (Exod. ch. 35), thus implying that even the Tabernacle could not be constructed on the Sabbath. The construction of the Tabernacle and its furnishings involved wool shearing, bleaching, hackling, spinning and weaving, moving from domain to domain, etc. Thus, the thirty-nine categories of work listed by the Mishna are based on what was regarded as work during the Torah days. The ban on trading is mentioned in Amos, Isaiah and Nehemiah. The prohibition of moving 2000 cubits outside one's city is implied in the verse, "Let no man go out from his place" (Exod. 16:29), which necessarily meant an area larger than one's home, for the men who discovered the wood gatherer were outside their own homes, without apparently breaking the law. (Dr. Yehiel Michael Gutman HaKohen, SEFER HASHABBAT, pp. 145-150)

5. SHABBAT, 2a.

The Mishna uses the example of the house master giving something to a poor man to indicate, as was pointed out by some commentators, that even in this instance, to perform a good deed, carrying from private to public domain is forbidden.

6. TOSAFOT states, "It appears that a *r'shut harabim* must have 600,000 persons traverse it, as in the desert." (*Shabbat*, 66a) However, the entire discussion in the Talmud seems to contravert this opinion. In *Shabbat* (98a) Rav says, He who carries something four *amot* in a *r'shut harabim* covered with rafters is *patur* (that is, he does not transgress a Torah law) for it is not like the Israelite camp in the desert. Nothing is said here about 600,000 persons.
7. TOSEPHTA, *Shabbat*, 1:1; *Shabbat*, 6a
   Rabbinically, one may not move a thing from a *carmelit* to a private domain.
8. SHABBAT, 2a, 3a, 5a.
   To be a transgressor, the thing's removal (*akirah*) and placement (*hanahah*) must be from and on an area of four *tephahim*. According to Rava, a man's hand is regarded as an area of four *tephahi*m by four. One is a transgressor if the thing he throws lands in another's hand; but if the recipient moves to receive it, the thrower is not *hayav,* since he did not make the *hanahah*. One who throws something which lands on an extremely high pole also transgresses, for a private domain has no height limit. (SHABBAT, 7b) However, if one rolls a bundle of rods, he does not transgress unless he lifted it up and carried it four *amot.* (SHABBAT, 8b)
9. SHABBAT, 2a
10. The bulk of a dry fig is regarded as a quantity of sufficient value, for many foods.
11. MISHNA, *Shabbat,* chapters 7-9.
12. SHABBAT, 78a.
    Rashi explains that parchment is expensive and is not used for receipts.
13. SHABBAT, 93b; TOSEPHTA, *Shabbat,* 9:11
14. SHABBAT, 90a
15. SHABBAT, 92a
16. *Ibid.*
17. *Loc. cit.*
18. *Ibid.,* 57a, 58a
19. TOSEPHTA, *Shabbat,* 6:7; MISHNA *Shabbat,* 63a
    The rabbis quote Isaiah's prophecy, "And they shall beat their swords into plowshares" to bolster their view that

weapons are not ornaments, but only shameful necessities.

20. SHABBAT, 96a

According to Rabbi Akiva, when a thrown thing passes through a *r'shut harabim* it is as if it rested there, which means that the thrower threw it from a private to a public domain. (*Shabbat*, 4a)

21. TOSEPHTA, *Shabbat,* 11:6-7
22. ERUVIN, 44b
23. YERUSHALMI, *Shabbat,* 19:1
24. SHABBAT, 31b
25. TOSEPHTA, *Shabbat,* 12:3
26. YERUSHALMI, *Shabbat,* 16:7
27. Rabbi Jonathan deduces this from the Torah's specific ban on making a fire. The Torah teaches us, he says, that every unit of work done on the Sabbath is a separate transgression as is making a fire.

MEKHILTA, *Shabbata,* 2

28. However, both the removal of baked bread and the sounding of the *shofar* are forbidden by rabbinic decree. (SHABBAT, 3b, 117a; ROSH HASHANAH 29b)
29. TOSEPHTA, *Shabbat,* 3:3
30. MAKKOT, 20b
31. SHABBAT, 105a, b
32. KREITUT, 19b
33. SHABBAT, 102b; YERUSHALMI, *Shabbat,* 7:2

In the *Yerushalmi* we find the following discussion: "What building was there in the Tabernacle? They (the Levites) placed boards on the (Tabernacle) thresholds." It was asked, "Was it not of a temporary nature?" Said Rabbi Yose, "Since it was done by command of God, it was as of a permanent nature." Said Rabbi Yose ben Rabbi Bon, "Since God promised to bring them (the Israelites) into the Land, the building was not of a permanent nature; and therefore building for a time (that will last only a while) is regarded work," which makes its doer a transgressor.

34. TOSEPHTA, *Shabbat,* 12:1
35. SHABBAT, 107a
36. *Ibid.,* 73b, 81a
37. *Ibid.,* 95a
38. *Ibid.,* 94b, 95a

39. *Ibid.,* 47a; DEUTERONOMY RABBAH, 3:1
    In the *Yerushalmi* (*Shabbat,* ch. 12) it is stated that since it is forbidden to put the menorah together, one must not handle it on the Sabbath, lest it will come apart, and he will put it together.
40. YERUSHALMI, *Shabbat,* 20:1
41. MEKHILTA, *Shabbata,* 1; SHABBAT, 105a
42. SIFRA, *Vayikra;* SHABBAT, 103a; TOSEPHTA, *Shabbat,* 12:5
43. SIFRA, *loc. cit.*
44. SHABBAT, 104b
45. TOSEPHTA, *Shabbat,* 12:7
46. *Ibid.,* 12:2; SHABBAT, 48a
47. TOSEPHTA, *Shabbat,* 3:6
48. SHABBAT, 73b
49. *Ibid.,* 95a
    According to the rabbis, these activities are rabbinic prohibitions, because of *sh'vut.*
50. SHABBAT, 143b
    Juice that oozes out of fruit kept for eating is permissible, but not if kept for the juice; therefore, the juice oozing out of olives and grapes is forbidden.
51. SHABBAT, 105a, b
52. TOSEPHTA, *Shabbat,* 13:18
53. SHABBAT, 106b
54. TOSEPHTA, *Shabbat,* 13:5-6
55. *Ibid.,* 13:4; *Shabbat,* 106b
56. SHABBAT, 75a
57. *Ibid.,* 107b
58. *Ibid.,* 80b
59. MEKHILTA, *Shabbata,* 2; SIFRA, *Kedoshim, Lev.,* 19:31
60. SIFRA, *Aharei Mot;* SHABBAT, 131b
61. MEKHILTA, *Kaspa,* 3 (Exod. 23:12)

CHAPTER V

1. ROSH HASHANAH, 29b; MEGILLAH, 4b
   However, according to Rabbi Yoseph, the *megillah* is not read on the Sabbath in order not to disappoint the poor

who will not receive the gifts they expect when the *megillah* is read.

2. SHABBAT, 11a; *Mishna,* 1:3; *Tosephta,* 1:5
3. SHABBAT, 57a; *Mishna,* 6:3

"Why is a woman forbidden to go out with ornaments (that she might remove)?" asks the Talmud Yerushalmi. Rabbi Ba answered, "Because women are ostentatious," and the ornament wearer might remove her ornament to show it to a friend, and then forgetfully carry the article four *amot* in the *r'shut harabim.* (YERUSHALMI, *Shabbat,* 6:1)

Since a woman is not inclined to show off her silver ornaments, Rabbi Yirmeyahu was advised by Rabbi Zeira not to forbid his young neighbors to wear their silver jewelry. Moreover, they might disobey such a prohibition; hence, even if wearing such jewelry should not be proper, it would be preferable that they be unwitting (not having been warned) transgressors. (YERUSHALMI, *loc. cit.*)

4. SHABBAT, 64b, 65a; *Mishna,* 6:5

Compare Rashi's explanation for the permissibility of a silver tooth with the *Yerushalmi's* lenience toward silver jewelry, mentioned in the preceding note.

5. SHABBAT, 62a; *Tosephta,* 5:10

Rabbi Meir considers these articles as burdens, and hence forbidden by the Torah; the sages consider them ornaments which the woman might remove to show them to a friend; but according to Rabbi Eliezer they are ornaments which she will not remove, for such articles are worn only by women with bad odor, and these will not remove their perfume aids. A similar difference of opinion applies to the wearing of a "golden city" crown. To Rabbi Meir, it is an article of burden, and therefore its wearer commits a Torah transgression; to the sages it is an ornament that the woman might remove, and hence she is rabbinically forbidden to go out with it; but according to Rabbi Eliezer, a "golden city" is an ornament which only an important woman can afford, and such a woman does not remove her ornaments to show to friends. (SHABBAT, 59b)

According to Rav, whenever the sages forbade going out with something into the *r'shut harabim,* it is also forbidden to go out with it into the courtyard, lest the wearer get used to it, and go out with it also into the *r'shut harabim,* except that a woman may go out into the courtyard with a foreign strand and a *kvul* (a kind of hairnet). According to Rabbi Ananni ben Rabbi Sasson, all ornaments may be worn when going out into the courtyard. Tosafot comments that the law is in accordance with Rabbi Ananni since this is also the opinion of Rabbi Yishmael ben Rabbi Yose, who is a *Tanna,* and because we follow the less rigorous opinion where rabbinical prohibition is involved. Moreover, Tosafot adds, "We who do not have a real *r'shut harabim,* but *carmeliot,* for our streets are not sixteen *amot* wide, and there are no 600,000 persons traversing them, our women may wear rings and jewels outside . . . and it is better that they be *shogegot* (unwitting transgressors, if they are not forbidden) than *mezidot* (knowing transgressors, if they are told not to wear them, and yet they do)." (SHABBAT, 64b)

We have already mentioned that in our view the opinion of Tosafot is not borne out by the general talmudic trend of discussion of this subject. Maimonides, in explaining *ir shel rabim* says, "a city of many people." He does not specify 600,000 persons. Rashi comments, "Some say, a city of 600,000." (ERUVIN, 59a; *Mishna,* ch. 5)

6. SHABBAT, 57a; *Mishna,* 6:1
7. SHABBAT, 60a; *Mishna,* 6:2

Rabbi Safra explained that it is forbidden to go out with phylacteries even according to the *Tanna* who teaches that one should put on *tefillin* on the Sabbath, lest he remove and carry them four *amot* in the *r'shut harabim.* However, according to all, the *tefillin* are like garments, and their wearer does not commit a Torah transgression. (SHABBAT, 61a)

According to another *Tanna* even women who find *tefillin* in the field may put them on and bring them to a safe place, for Sabbath and night are a time for *tefillin,* and women, too, are required to put them on, and therefore they may carry them back. (SHABBAT, 62a; *Tosephta,* 8:10)

8. ERUVIN, *Mishna,* 1:6-9
9. SHABBAT, *Mishna,* 11:2
10. ERUVIN, 90a

11. SHABBAT, *Mishna*, 3:3

According to the Gemara, heating with a sun derivative is worse than heating it with sun heat, for one may confuse the former with the derivative of fire heat. Therefore, one may heat cold water with sun rays, but one may not poach an egg within a sun-heated cloth. (SHABBAT, 39a)

12. SHABBAT, *Tosephta*, 3:6

In the Gemara, the version is that Rabban Shimeon permits it on a heated roof but not in heated lime (lest one come to put it also in hot ashes).

13. SHABBAT, *Mishna*, 3:3

14. YERUSHALMI, *Shabbat*, 3:3

15. SHABBAT, 41b

16. SHABBAT, *Tosephta*, 1:9

17. YERUSHALMI, *Shabbat*, 18:1

18. SHABBAT, 18a

The Gemara explains that according to Beit Shammai one is required to rest also his vessels *(shvitat kelim)*, but according to Beit Hillel one is required to give rest only to his animals since the latter are living beings. The Gemara explains further that Beit Shammai permit the burning of a candle and the keeping of a pot on a stove because, for that purpose, the religious court *(beit din)* renders them ownerless—a necessary legal fiction (according to this view). The Yerushalmi, however, gives a more logical reason. It states that Beit Shammai permit the burning of a candle because the work is in the kindling, and that was completed when the candle was lit; and the pot is permitted to be left on the stove only for the retention of heat. (By the way, it seems that whenever the Bavli and Yerushalmi differ, the latter is more reasonable and simpler, bearing out the famous comparison by Rabbi Yirmiyahu of the Babylonian Talmud to the dark places.) (SANHEDRIN, 24a)

19. SHABBAT, *Mishna*, 1:5-6

20. *Ibid.*, 1:1-11

21. *Ibid.*, 1:9

The Gemara explains that elsewhere Beit Shammai forbid self-completing work, lest he will come to complete it, and commit a Torah transgression. Here, even if he should come to squeeze the fruit with his hands, he will not commit a Torah transgression, and hence Beit Shammai, too, did not institute a precautionary ban or *g'zeira*. This reason is additional to the one given concerning *shvitat kelim*, as explained in note 18. (SHABBAT, 19a)

22. SHABBAT, *Mishna*, 1:10
23. SHABBAT, *Tosephta*, 1:11
    According to this source, spices may be placed on coal on Friday, although their perfuming process will go on the entire Sabbath. Water pipes may be opened into the garden on Sabbath eve, and allowed to run a whole day.
24. SHABBAT, *Mishna*, 153; Yerushalmi quoted in Rav Nissim Gaon commentary.
25. SHABBAT, *Tosephta*, 15:15; YERUSHALMI, 6:1
26. SHABBAT, 147a; *Mishna*, 22:5
27. SHABBAT, *Tosephta*, 18:17; BEITZA, 36b
28. SHABBAT, *Tosephta*, 4:10
29. *Ibid.*, 13:9
30. SHABBAT, *Mishna*, 22:3
31. PESAHIM, 47b
    Fragment of a Zadokite Work requires that the food be prepared also for all its beneficiaries. It states: "One shall (not) eat or drink unless he was in the camp (on Friday)." (*Edah v'Edut*, pp. 113-115)
32. *M'vatel keli m'heikhano* (SHABBAT, 42b, 43a; MISHNA, 3:6)
33. *Muktza mahamat issur.* (*Ibid.*, 44a) According to *Tosafot* (45b), lighting it on the Sabbath was like pushing away the permissibility with one's hands. Rav was once asked whether a Hanukah menorah could be removed on the Sabbath if one feared a visit by the Magi (who forbade the use of fire). He answered that it is permissible, for in time of danger Rabbi Shimeon's opinion, permitting the handling of an extinguished lamp, was acceptable.
34. *Muktza mahamat mius.* (Ibid., 44a)
35. SHABBAT, 112b; *Mishna*, 17:1-4
36. *Muktza mahamat hissaron kis* (SHABBAT, 157a)
37. SHABBAT, 143a; *Mishna*, 21:3
38. *Ibid.*, 142b; *Mishna*, 21:1-2
39. HULIN, 15b
40. SHABBAT, 128b

41. *Loc. cit.;* BEITZA, 2a
42. MEKHILTA, *Shabbata,* 1
43. SHABBAT, *Mishna,* 24:2-3; *Tosephta,* 15:13
44. SHABBAT, *Mishna,* 23:3-4; *Tosephta,* 18:7
45. SHABBAT, *Tosephta,* 15, 16
46. SHABBAT, *Mishna,* 18:1, 2
47. SIFRA, *Aharei Mot;* SHABBOT, *Tosephta,* 18:17
48. SHABBAT, *Tosephta,* 14:7
49. *Ibid.,* 14:12, 13
50. AVODAH ZARAH, 22a
52. SHABBAT, *Mishna,* 16:6-8
53. *Ibid.,* 23:4
54. BABA KAMA, 80a
    Tosafot comments that for the performance of the *mitz-vah* of *yishuv Eretz Yisrael* this is permissible. Of course, the rabbis permitted the setting aside of the restrictions of *sh'vut* for the performance of other *mitzvot,* especially those concerning the community, as pointed out elsewhere.
55. SHABBAT, *Tosephta,* 17:14
56. SHABBAT, *Mishna,* 24:1
57. PESAHIM, 51a
    When Rav lectured to his students, he ruled like Rabbi Meir (that one who erred and cooked on the Sabbath may eat of it) ; but when he lectured to the people, on the Sabbath, he ruled like Rabbi Yehudah (that one may not eat of food cooked in error on the Sabbath until after the Sabbath is over, and one would have had sufficient time to cook it), lest the uneducated abuse a lenient ruling, and become lax in observance. (HULIN, 15a)
58. SHABBAT, 153b, *Gemara* and *Rashi;* 51b, *Gemara* and *Tosafot*
59. SHABBAT, *Mishna,* 5:1, 2, 4
    According to Rabbi Yehudah ben Pazi, the rabbis said to Rabbi Eliezer ben Azariah, "Remove the band, or you will be excommunicated." Rabbi Hananiah said it happened only once, and in repentance Rabbi Eliezer fasted so often that his teeth turned black. Rabbi Eidi said that the cow belonged to his wife. The rabbis of Babylonia explained that the cow belonged to a neighbor; and because Rabbi Eliezer did not reprimand the neighbor, he was blamed. SHABBAT, 54b; YERUSHALMI, 5:4)

60. SHABBAT, *Yerushalmi*, 17:1
61. George F. Moore, JUDAISM, Vol. II, p. 30
     Dr. Moore here expresses an idea similar to one found
in the Talmud. In *Hagigah* (chap. 1), the Mishna states,
"The laws of the Sabbath ... are like mountains suspended
by a hair, little scripture and many laws." Some scholars,
erroneously, interpret this to mean that the many Sabbath
restrictions have little scriptural basis. It seems very unlikely
that the Mishna would disparage the basis of the laws, and
thus weaken unconditional adherence to them. The Gemara
explains (*Hagigah*, 10 a,b) that although the Torah does
not specify intended work, the rabbis inferred from the
Torah's adjoining the commands to observe the Sabbath
and to construct the Tabernacle, where work had to be
designed, that one does not transgress the Sabbath, according to the Torah, unless he intends to do the work which
he does. That this is really the meaning of the Mishna is
evident from its initial statement, which reads, "The (sages')
power to release from vows are flights in the air, and do
not have what to lean on." Likewise, the following statement means that while the sages did not release one who
did unintended work from a feeling of transgression, they
did free him from feeling that he committed a Torah transgression, which would carry a far deeper guilt and graver
atonement.
62. SHABBAT, 153a, *Gemara* and *Tosafot*
     The Gemara explains that if possible, he gives it to a
non-Jew, and he does not put it on his animal, because he
is commanded to give rest to his animal. However, if his
companion happens to be a demented or minor Jew then
he places his purse on his animal, for although they are not
subject to the Torah law, they are Jews and passers-by
could confuse them with adult, sane Jews.
63. SHABBAT, 43b
64. SHABBAT, *Mishna*, 6:6-7
65. *Ibid.*, 6:10
66. SHABBAT, 41b; *Mishna*, ch. 4; *Tosephta*, 3:2, 4:12
     One must not cover up warm food on the Sabbath, lest
he put it in the ashes and rake the coal, but he may add
covers to already covered food.

67. *Ibid.*
68. SHABBAT, *Mishna,* 14:3-4
69. *Ibid.,* 14:2
70. SHABBAT, *Tosephta,* 13:18
71. *Ibid.,* 4:14
73. *Ibid.,* 13:9
72. *Ibid.,* 6:3-6
74. KETUBOT, 3b, 4b

The groom is a *m'kalkel,* which Rabbi Yehudah does not regard as a transgression, and although making a wound is a main Sabbath transgression, here (when they are together for the first time) it is an unintended act, which Rabbi Shimeon does not regard a transgression. (*Ibid.,* 6a,b; BERAKHOT, *Yerushalmi,* 2:6)

75. SHABBAT, 120b

As explained by Rava and Abbaye, even Rabbi Shimeon who says that an unintended act is not a transgression agrees that it is forbidden in instances of, "Scalp it; will it not die?"; that is, where the unintended result is inevitable. Here, too, the draft will surely put out the lamp.

76. SHABBAT, *Mishna,* 15:3
77. SHABBAT, *Mishna,* 22:3; *Tosephta,* 17:9; *Yerushalmi,* 22:3
78. SHABBAT, *Tosephta,* 13:18-19

The Rabban Gamliel household did not fold their linens on the Sabbath, because they had other sets for the day. Rashi explains that to fold linens is to smooth out creases, which is like mending them. (SHABBAT, 113a)

79. SHABBAT, *Mishna,* 23:1, 2
80. SHABBAT, *Tosephta,* 18:2

The official proclamations may be read, probably, because such reading concerns one's safety.

81. *Ibid.,* 4:4
82. SHABBAT, 40a
83. YEVAMOT, 46b

The mending is of the person (*m'taken gavra*).

One who bathes in the warm waters of Tiberias may shower himself, but he must not have others shower him. (SHABBAT, *Tosephta,* 17:13)

84. SHABBAT, *Tosephta,* 4:2, 3
85. *Ibid.,* 17:16

86. ERUVIN, 100b
87. SHABBAT, *Tosephta,* 14:3, 4
88. SHABBAT, *Mishna,* 16:1-3
89. *Ibid.,* 16:4-7

CHAPTER VI

1. MEKHILTA, *Shabbata,* 2

    Moreover, even construction of the Tabernacle was forbidden on the Sabbath, as cited in an earlier section. *(Ibid.; Sifra, Kedoshim)*

2. YEVAMOT, 21b

    Rabbi Hiyya explains it as follows: Sabbath work is forbidden to all; therefore, the Torah's permission of work in the Temple was given not to all (as asserted by Rabbi Shimeon) but only to *kohanim.* (This means that permission was given only to the designated persons in the designated place.)

3. MEKHILTA, *Shabbata,* 1

    From the verse, "He who desecrates it shall be put to death" (Exod. 31:14) Rabbi Yehudah infers that it is a transgression to desecrate it even for a fleeting moment *(heref ayin).* One must strive to keep the Sabbath, even if only the smallest possible area of observance is left.

4. MEKHILTA, *Shabbata,* 2

    Permission to kindle a fire in the Temple is also derived from the verse, "Do not kindle a fire in your dwelling places" (Exod. 35:3), implying that in God's dwelling place, the Temple, it is permissible.

5. SIFRA, *Tzav*
6. *Ibid., Emor*
7. PESAHIM, 66a
8. *Ibid.*

    Hillel reasoned that there was more justification for offering the paschal lamb in its due season, including the Sabbath, than for the two daily public sacrifices *(korban tamid);* for failure to offer the paschal lamb entailed the *karet* (ostracism) penalty, whereas failure to offer the *tamid* did not entail that penalty. Hillel's opinion, however, was accepted only after he stated that his was also his teachers' opinion.

After Hillel was appointed head of the *Sanhedrin,* it happened that the people forgot to bring their knives on Friday for the slaughter of the paschal lamb. Hillel was asked what to do. He replied that he had forgotten the ruling, but that the people would probably do the right thing on the Sabbath, the day when the lambs were to be offered, for "if they are not prophets, they are children of prophets." On the day of the Sabbath, the people stuck their knives into the wool of their lambs, or between the horns of the goats, and thus brought their knives to the Temple. (Carrying on the Sabbath in an irregular way *(kilahar yad)* is forbidden only rabbinically, and in the case of a public *mitzvah,* it is permitted.) When Hillel saw what the people did, he recalled that it was what his teachers taught. *(Loc. cit.)*

9. PESAHIM, *Mishna,* 6:1
10. *Ibid.,* 65b

Bringing the lamb through the public domain *(r'shut harabim),* although forbidden only by rabbinic law, for "the living carries itself," is nevertheless forbidden by Rabbi Akiva, since it could have been done before the Sabbath. Rabbi Akiva arrives at his opinion as follows: Sprinkling an unclean person *(tameh met),* whose seventh day on which he has to bathe occurs on a Sabbath, is not allowed, although the sprinkling is forbidden only by rabbinic law (for it is not work, but only appears as making fit, or mending, the person—*m'taken gavra),* and although without the sprinkling the unclean person will not be able to partake of the paschal sacrifice. Rabbi Eliezer, however, rejects Rabbi Akiva's view in this, too.

According to Rabbi Eliezer the slaughtering and its accessories supersede the Sabbath, but according to Rabbi Akiva, the accessories do not supersede the Sabbath for they could have been done before the Sabbath. Rabbi Eliezer argued: The burnt parts *(eimurim)* of the public sacrifices *(t'midim)* are offered on the Sabbath although they could wait until after the Sabbath. Now, what difference is there between the accessories which succeed the slaughtering and those which precede it? Rabbi Akiva retorted: Once the slaughtering supersedes the Sabbath, the succeeding accessories can do likewise. But to allow the accessory things preceding the slaughtering is to risk desecrating the Sabbath in vain, for something ritually unfit (*p'sul*) might be found in the slaughtering, and all the preceding acts will not be part of a justified Sabbath dispensation. For this reason, the accessories preceding the circumcision are also forbidden lest the child become sick, causing the circumcision to be postponed, and everything preceding it will have become unjustified Sabbath desecrations. (PESAHIM, *Tosephta,* ch. 5; *Yerushalmi,* 19:1)

11. SIFRA, *Tzav* (*Lev.* 6:14)
12. MINAHOT, 96a; *Mishna,* ch. 11
13. *Ibid.,* 49a
14. *Ibid.,* 72a, b
15. *Ibid.,* 65a, b

To emphasize the Pharisaic rejection of the Sadducee interpretation and practice, the ceremony of cutting the *omer* was dramatized. Delegates of the religious court (*beit din*) went out to the field on the eve of Passover, and tied the barley stalks which were still in the ground. The people of all nearby villages gathered so that the harvest could be carried out impressively. On the eve of the second day of Passover, after dark, the reaper asked three times, "Has the sun set?" and each time he was answered, "Yes." Then he asked, three times, "With the sickle?" and again he was answered each time, "Yes." (All questions and answers were repeated three times.) He asked, "In this basket?" and the answer came, "Yes." Then he asked, "On the Sabbath?" and he was answered, "Yes."

16. SIFRA, *Emor, Behar;* SHABBAT, 131a; SUCCAH, 43a; YOMA, 66a; ERUVIN, *Tosephta,* 8:12
17. MINAHOT, 100b; MEKHILTA, *Pis'ha,* 5; SIFREI, *Beha'-alotkha;* PESAHIM, 69b, 70b
18. SIFREI, *Pinhas* (Numbers 28:9, 10); YOMA, 50a; T'MU-RAH, *Tosephta,* ch. 1
19. SIFRA, *Emor;* ROSH HASHANAH, 21b
20. ROSH HASHANAH, 21b; *Mishna,* 1:4
21. MINAHOT, 64a; ROSH HASHANAH, *Mishna,* 1:5

If one of the witnesses was unable to walk, he was placed on a donkey, even with his bed. The witnesses were allowed to arm themselves for their protection. If they were distant from the court, they were allowed to take along provision for twenty-four hours, but not for longer, for by then the month would have become sanctified even without their testimony. (ROSH HASHANAH, 22a, *Mishna,* 1:9)

22. SIFRA, *Tazria*

One rabbi infers from the verse, "On the eighth day you shall circumcize the flesh of his foreskin" (Lev. 12:3) — *even on the Sabbath.* Ula says circumcision on the eighth day, including the Sabbath, is a tradition. (SHABBAT, 132a)

23. YEVAMOT, 64b

24. SHABBAT, 131b, 133a; *Mishna,* 18:3, 19:1, 2

In the *Yerushalmi,* one of the rabbis consulted concerning the forgotten knife remarked, "Of entertainment (the spiced wine) you did not forget to bring, but the knife you forgot; let it (the circumcision) be postponed."

25. ERUVIN, *Tosephta,* 3:7

26. NUMBERS RABBAH, 23:1

27. ERUVIN, 45a

28. SHABBAT, 19a; ERUVIN, *Tosephta,* 3:1

29. SHABBAT, 121b

30. MEKHILTA, *Shabbata,* 1

31. SHABBAT, *Tosephta,* 18:11

32. YOMA, 85a; SHABBAT, *Tosephta,* 15:13, 14

The Tosephta states that Rabbi Akiva supported the principle that even possible danger to life supersedes the Sabbath, as follows: The Temple service supersedes the Sabbath, and yet the service is set aside if there is a possibility of saving a life; surely, the Sabbath should be set aside if thus there is a chance of saving a life. The Gemara elaborates this proof: According to the Torah, a *kohen* who shed blood cannot seek refuge at the altar (Exod. 21:14); however, if he already started to officiate, he was allowed to complete the sacrifice. On the other hand, a *kohen* who knew evidence which *possibly* could save another person convicted to death, was requested to leave even in the middle of a service, in order to testify. Thus, even the possibility of saving a life superseded the service. Surely, Rabbi Akiva reasoned, the chance of saving a life should supersede the Sabbath.

"And he shall live by them" (Exod. 15:5); nothing takes precedence over life except resistance to idolatry, adultery and bloodshed. However, in time of religious persecution (when example has the power to bolster or demoralize), one should give his life rather than transgress any *mitzvah*, as Scripture teaches, "And they shall not profane My name, and I shall be sanctified in the midst of the Children of Israel, for I the Lord sanctify you" (Exod. 22:32); and, "God fashioned all for His sake" (Proverbs 16:4). (Shabbat, *Tosephta*, 15:13, 14; Yoma, 38a)

33. YOMA, 84b, 85a; *Mishna*, 8:7
34. SHABBAT, *Tosephta*, 16:12; YOMA, *Loc. cit.*
35. YOMA, *Mishna*, 8:6, AVODAH ZARA, 28a; TANHUMA, *Jethro*
36. AVODAH ZARA, 28b
   It is permissible to grind up the medicinal ingredients where the ailment may possibly endanger life; but the medicine must be curative. (YOMA, 49b)
37. MINAHOT, 64a
38. SHABBAT, 128b, 134b, *Mishna*, 18:3
39. ARAKHIN, 7a
40. MEKHILTA, *Nizakin*, 3
   Although the Temple service which supersedes the Sabbath is not allowed to proceed if the *kohen* is a murderer (who sought shelter at the altar), nevertheless the Sabbath is not set aside in order to mete out capital punishment. (The Sabbath is set aside to save life but not to take it, even in the name of justice, for that can be executed a day later. But meanwhile the murderer is not allowed to participate in the service, for his officiating would be abhorrent to God.)
   Although the Temple service is also set aside to bury a *met mitzvah* (a deceased without relatives or friends), the Sabbath is not set aside for that purpose.

CHAPTER VII

1. ZEVAHIM, *Mishna*, 10:1; HORAYOT, *Mishna*, ch. 10; YERUSHALMI, *Shekalim*, 3:4

2. PESAHIM, 58a

The Gemara explains that the roasting of the paschal sacrifice does not supersede the Sabbath; therefore, the *Tamid* is offered earlier when Passover comes on a Sabbath. Rashi comments that roasting does not supersede the Sabbath because it is a layman's need, and it can be done before sundown.

3. EZRA, 6:18; II CHRONICLES, 7:6, 8:14; TAMID, *Mishna*, 1:1, with Maimonides' Commentary; Yaavetz, TOLDOT ISRAEL, Vol. III, Note 6

4. TAANIT, 26a, 27a, b

5. YERUSHALMI, *Eruvin*, 10:12

6. ROSH HASHANAH, 31a

7. SANHEDRIN, 22b

8. SUCCAH, 50b, 51a

9. *Ibid.*, 53b

10. SIFRA, *Emor*

11. SUCCAH, 41b

12. *Ibid.*, 48a

13. MEGILLAH, 5a

The Yerushalmi explains that the *Hakhel* was postponed till Sunday because of the need to construct a *bimah* from which the king read, and that could not be constructed on the Sabbath. (YERUSHALMI, *Megillah*, 1:6)

14. "Why is the Sabbath called 'holy assembly'?" asks Nahmanides, and answers, "For all were required to sanctify it by assembling in God's house." (Lev. 23:2-3) Already in pre-Temple I days we find references to visits to godly men or holy places on the Sabbath, festivals and in times of great need. This is seen directly or implicitly in the following: Gen. 25:22; Exod. 33:7, ch. 40; Lev. 1:1, etc.,; Deut. 17:8-12, 18:18; Josh. 8:30-35; I Samuel 9:9-14; II Kings 4:23; Isaiah 1:10-17; Jeremiah ch. 7; Malachi ch. 2. From the Kings reference Rabbi Itzhak infers that one should visit his teacher on the new moon and Sabbath. (SUCCAH, 27b)

15. SHIR HASHIRIM RABBAH, ch. 5

16. YALKUT SHIMONI, *Va-yakhel*, (*Ex.*, 35:1)

17. MEGILLAH, 29b; Wolfson, PHILO pp. 95-96

18. MEGILLAH, 32b; SOFERIM 10:7

That ten constitute a quorum for the declaration of God's holiness in public the Gemara infers from the Torah's application of the word *edah*—community—to the ten spies. Tosafot, in *Megillah,* quotes the Yerushalmi that it is permissible to continue the service if one of the ten left before the conclusion, but he who leaves is blameworthy.

19. MEGILLAH, 21a,b, 23a

The reason for seven to read on Sabbath morning and three on Sabbath afternoon is contained in the following underlying rule: Where work stoppage is involved, as on week days, a fast day and Sabbath *minha,* which is close to the end of the Sabbath (and also because the people have already spent the entire day in listening to lectures on *halakha*—Rashi) only three read; on *Rosh Hodesh* and *Hol Hamoed,* where only partial work stoppage is involved (for women do not work, and men work less on *Hol Hamoed,* and besides on those days there is also the *Musaph* service) four read; on the festivals five read because they are days of rest; on Yom Kippur six read because of its higher holiness as indicated by the punishment, *karet,* meted out to its transgressor; and on the Sabbath seven read because of its highest holiness as indicated by the punishment of stoning given to a warned transgressor. Rabbi Akiva reverses the numbers of readers for Sabbath and Yom Kippur. (MEGILLAH, 21a,b, 22b, 23a; TOSEPHTA, ch. 3) According to Acts (XIII:14-16), when the reading from the Prophets was concluded there followed a message, which visitors were invited to deliver, if they desired to do so.

20. MEGILLAH, 23a, 24b; SOFERIM, 15:15
21. GITTIN, 59b
22. *Ibid.,* 60a
23. MEGILLAH, 23b, 32a
24. *Ibid.,* 21b

Rashi explains that the translation was for illiterates and women who did not understand Hebrew; "and the *Targum* is the vernacular of the Babylonians" (Jews of Babylonia).

25. *Ibid.,* 32a
26. SOFERIM, 11:1

The *Tur,* quoted by the *Nahalat Yaakov* commentary on

Soferim, states that today, when everyone called up recites both blessings, it is not necessary for the reader to sit down between readings.
27. MEGILLAH, 24a
28. *Ibid.,* 23b
Rashi explains that the number of verses was decreased when an interpreter was present in order to lessen the burden on the congregation. *Ibid.,* 32a
Apparently this statement was made to encourage a congregant to accept *g'lillah.*
30. SOFERIM, 14:14
31. MEGILLAH, 29a
According to Rav, the Torah reading for *Parshat Sh'kalim* is from ch. 28 in Numbers, but according to Shmuel it is from Exodus, ch. 30 (as it is today). The Gemara seeks to bolster Shmuel's view by quoting the Tosephta (ch. 3) where it is stated that the reading for *Parshat Sh'kalim* may be read during two consecutive weeks, once in its regular cycle and the second time as the special reading, thus pointing to *Ki Tissa,* containing Exodus, ch. 30, as maintained by Shmuel. Then the Gemara weakens this proof by asserting that Rav could interpret the Tosephta in accordance with the Palestinian triennial Torah reading cycle, which makes it possible for *Pinhas,* containing the reading according to Rav, to come at the time of *Rosh Hodesh Adar,* when *Parshat Sh'kalim* would be read.
32. MEGILLAH, 21a,b
There is no *maftir,* Rashi explains, not to burden the people on work days, and at Sabbath *minha* which is close to the end of Sabbath.
33. SHABBAT, 24a, 116b
Rashi comments: "I found in a Gaonic responsum that they used to read from the Prophets at the Sabbath *minha* service, until it was prohibited by the Parthians. Once the custom ceased, it was not revived." The custom of reading from the Holy Writings was maintained in Nehardea, where Shmuel taught.
34. BABA KAMA, 113a
35. SHABBAT, *Mishna,* 16:1
Rashi, in explaining the Mishna writes: Rabbanu Halevi

said that even individuals should not read in the Holy
Writings, for it interfers with study (of *halakhah*), since the
Holy Writings draw the heart. On the Sabbath, lay people,
who were occupied the whole week, used to come and listen
to a lecture on ritual law. (*Shabbat*, 115a) However, in the
Tosephta, Rabbi Nehemiah gives a different reason for the
prohibition. He says that one must not read from Holy
Writings, to discourage the reading from secular documents,
for people will conclude, "If the Holy Writings may not be
read, surely these may not." (*Shabbat*, Tosephta, 14:1) The
prohibition of reading non-*halakhic* books did not apply
to studying them, for Rabbi Yohanan and Rabbi Shimeon
ben Lakish used to look into Aggada books on the Sabbath.
(*Gittin*, 60a)

Translated Holy Writings were, of course, forbidden, as
is evident from an incident related in the Tosephta. Once
Abba Halaphta saw Rabban Gamliel reading a translation
of Job. He said to him, "I remember Rabban Gamliel your
grandfather, who when he was brought a translation of Job
told the builder to put it under a row of bricks." Rabban
Gamliel (the grandson) then requested that the book be put
away. (Tosephta, *Shabbat*, 14:2)

The importance with which the rabbis regarded the
lectures on *halakhah* can be seen from the following two
selections: R. Zeira said: "At first, when I used to see the
rabbis run to the lecture on the Sabbath, I thought that
they were desecrating the Sabbath. But since I heard, in the
name of Rabbi Yehoshua ben Levi that at all times a man
should run to a *halakhah* lecture, even on the Sabbath, I
too run." (*Berakhot*, 6b)

M'reimar and Mar Zutra, on the Sabbaths of the *Kallah*
(before the three festivals—Rashi) used to assemble ten
men for services, and at the conclusion, went to lecture.
(This enabled them to continued the lecture, without an
interruption.) *Ibid.*, 30a

36. LEVITICUS RABBAH, 9:9; NUMBERS RABBAH, 9:20
37. Wolfson, PHILO, pp. 95-96
38. SEFER HASHABBAT, pp. 14-17
39. Philo, PHILOSOPHICAL WRITINGS, p. 44
40. YERUSHALMI, *Berakhot*, ch. 4; *Pesikta*, 23:2; BAVLI,
Berakhot, 27a,b

According to Rava, the incident happened before the rabbinic decree against entering a steam bath on the Sabbath, for, although Rabbi Yehudah Hanassi prayed early *by mistake*, nevertheless, it constituted a reception of the Sabbath, and if the steam bath had already been prohibited by the rabbis, he would not have entered it.

41. *Ibid.*

Avidan told that once when it became cloudy on a Saturday the people thought that the Sabbath had ended, and they prayed *maariv*. Then the clouds lifted, and the sun began to shine. When Rabbi Yehudah was asked what the people should do, he said that they need not pray again. The Gemara rules that this does not apply to individuals but only to a congregation, for we do not trouble them unnecessarily; but even they were not permitted to work until the Sabbath was really over. According to the Yerushalmi, Rabbi Yehudah Hanassi instructed his Amora to preach that it is permissible but according to the Babylonian Talmud he taught that the prayers need not be repeated after the Sabbath.

One who forgot to pray *minha* on Friday, prays two Sabbath *amidot* on Sabbath evening. (*Berakhot,* 26a)

42. SHABBAT, 119a
42. SHABBAT, 119a
43. *Ibid.,* 119b

Tosafot comments: The *Vayekhulu* is recited in the *Kiddush* as well as in the *Amidah* in order to enable one's family to fulfil their duty, too. It is also said aloud after the repetition of the partial *Amidah* on festivals occurring on the Sabbath, when it is not said during the silent *Amidah*. It was instituted to be said on non-festival Sabbaths, too, although it has already been said during the *Amidah,* not to distinguish between Sabbath and Sabbath. *Tosaphot, Pesahim,* 106a

Eliezer Levy, in his *Yesodot Hatefillah* (pp. 191-192), quotes the Talmud that he who recites the *Vayekhulu* is blessed by the two angels who accompany him home from the synagogue with the forgiveness of his sins. Levy explains that the "men of the stations" (*anshei hamaamadot*), whose recitation of the chapters dealing with the sacrifices led to the forgiveness of sins, concluded their weekly reading of Genesis ch. 1 with the opening passage in ch. 2 (*Vayekhulu*). However, it seems to us that the emphasis given to the reading of the passage on Friday evening—and the need to repeat it three times—was meant to counteract some sectarian view that the Sabbath did not start on Friday evening.

44. SHABBAT, 24b
45. PESAHIM, 100b

However, those who do not repeat the *Kiddush* at home must recite another blessing on wine, if they should drink it with their meal, whereas they who recite the *Kiddush* where they eat need not repeat the blessing when they drink wine with their meal.

46. PESAHIM, 100b, 101a

Tosafot comments: The guests fulfil the *mitzvah* of *Kiddush* even if only one tastes the wine, but preferably all should taste it. However, where there are no guests, *Kiddush* should not be recited, for it is a vain blessing (*b'rakhah l'vatalah*), for the law is in accordance with Shmuel that *Kiddush* should be recited only where there is a meal.

47. SHABBAT, 24a, b
48. MEGILLAH, 24b; HAGIGAH, 16a
49. *Ibid.*

CHAPTER VIII

1. AVOT DI RABBI NATHAN, 11:1
2. AVODAH ZARA, 3a
3. BEITZA, 16a. In the Yerushalmi version, Shammai bought wood for the Sabbath, at the beginning of the week. Concerning Hillel, the Yerushalmi says that he had a greater attitude (*midah*), for *all* his deeds were for the sake of Heaven.
4. YERUSHALMI, *Peah*, 8; PESIKTA, 23:1
5. TAANIT, 20b
6. KETUBOT, 67b
7. BEITZA, 15b, 16a; SHABBAT, 118a; PESAHIM, 112a
8. ERUVIN, 43b
9. BABA KAMA, 113a
10. SUCCAH, 44b

11. SHABBAT, 119a
12. HAGGIGA, 5a

The Gemara comments: "But Rava did send such meat:"; and answers that Rava knew that his wife, the daughter of Rabbi Hasdai, was trained to remove the veins and fats, and would do it even when busy with Sabbath preparations.

13. VAYIKRA RABBA, 23:6
14. SHABBAT, 33b
14. SHABBAT, 33b
15. BABA METZIA, 32a
16. SHABBAT, 31a

Hillel, as seen from the bettor's coming three times to anger him, started personal preparations for the Sabbath early.

17. *Ibid.*, 25b
18. GITIN, 52a
19. *Loc. cit.*
21. *Ibid.*, 14b

From the verse, "Let everyman stay in his place" (Exod. 16:29), the rabbis deduced that one must not go beyond two thousand cubits outside his city or his established resting place, if he is on the road, or has to be somewhere outside his city, in which case the "place" consists of four cubits. (*Mekhilta, Vayassa,* 6) Apparently, the rabbis felt that this extension of "place" was not contrary to the intent of the Torah, for in *Soferim* (14:18) it is stated that a *minhag* (custom) modifies a *halakha* only when it is well-founded, and then it becomes law, after its establishment. If the custom is without Torah support, it is only like an error in judgment, and cannot become law.

In connection with the two thousand cubit limit there is the interesting story in the Talmud about Rabbi Meir and his teacher the apostate Elisha. When Rabbi Meir was told that his former teacher was riding outside, he left the *beit midrash,* and went to Elisha, to talk with him. Elisha was riding, and Rabbi Meir was walking. When they reached the two thousand cubit limit, Elisha said, "Meir, return, for I have estimated by my horse trot that we have reached the Sabbath *t'hum.*" Rabbi Meir replied, "You, too, return." (*Haggiga,* 15a)

22. ERUVIN, 49b, 51b, 26b, 31b

One may not designate as his representative a person who rejects the principle of the *eruv.*

23. *Ibid.,* 58b, 80a

24. *Ibid.,* 80a

All participants in the *eruv* must believe in it. However, a Jew who does not desecrate the Sabbath *publicly* may "merge" his dwelling with other neighbors' for their benefit. (*Hulin,* 6a; *Eruvin,* 69b)

25. *Ibid,* 6a

26. *Ibid.,* 59a

A "private city" (one which is traversed by fewer than 600,000—Rashi) "which is made into a public one" (by the addition of apartments or market places—Rashi) with a *r'shut harabim* (a street or square sixteen *amot* wide) may also be covered by an *eruv,* by the placing of a board or rafter on either side. (*Loc. cit.*)

27. ERUVIN, 46b; YERUSHALMI, 3:2, 7:9. In the second source we find this illustration: A woman sent her son with food for the *eruv,* to the house of an unfriendly neighbor. The female neighbor, in whose house the *eruv* was placed, hugged and kissed the child. When he came home and told his mother, she said, "She loves me so much, and I did not know it"; and thus they became reconciled.

Rashi explains that in talmudic days the houses used to open into a courtyard, from where the dwellers used to go out to the street. The courtyard, therefore, was like a public domain. The rabbis required an *eruv,* to permit carrying from house to house. Every house in the yard contributed some bread, which was placed in one basket, in one house, and all participants became as dwellers of the house; and all houses became as one. (*Succa,* 3a)

28. MEKHILTA, *Vayassa,* 5

The *Mekhilta* infers from the verse, "And it shall be on the sixth day, and they shall prepare. . . ." Exod. 16:5) that on a weekday but not on a festival one should prepare for the Sabbath. However, one may prepare a dish on the

NOTES 175

eve of the festival, as an *eruv,* and it becomes the basis for
the permission to cook on the festival for the Sabbath. In
a discussion in the Gemara, Shmuel, using the verse, "Remember the Sabbath day to keep it holy" (Exodus 2:8),
as his text says: Remember it so that another day (a festival
coming on its eve) does not cause it to be forgotten. Rava
adds that one should select good food for the Sabbath as
well as for the festival. Rashi explains that the Torah surely
does not speak about *eruvei tavshillin,* but the rabbis use
the verses as texts, only. *(Beitza,* 15b)

Another reason for this kind of *eruv* is given in *Pesahim.* There the Talmud states that it should be permissible,
by Torah law, to cook on the festival for the Sabbath (as
it is for the festival itself), for both are "one holiness."
The rabbis, however, prohibited the cooking on a festival
for the Sabbath lest one be led to cook on the festival also
for a weekday. The *eruv,* however, makes a distinction.
(Pesahim, 46b)

29. BEITZA, 16b
30. PESAHIM, 50b
31. YERUSHALMI, *Shvi'it,* 1:1
32. SHABBAT, 12a
33. PESAHIM, 13a
34. SHABBAT, 35b

In connection with the dispute between Rabbi Nathan
and Rabbi Yehudah Hanassi it is apropos to cite the very
interesting incident told about Rabbi Eliezer. When he
became sick, Rabbi Akiva and his colleagues came to visit.
It was the eve of the Sabbath, and Hyrkanos, Rabbi
Eliezer's son, came in to remove his father's phylacteries.
Rabbi Eliezer reprimanded his son. The latter left, and
remarked to the visitors who were in the dining hall, "It
seems that my father's mind is confused." Overhearing,
Rabbi Eliezer remarked, "His and his mother's minds are
confused, for they leave a transgression involving the penalty of stoning (lighting candles after dark), and worry
about one (removing the phylacteries before the Sabbath)
forbidden only by the rabbis." *(Sanhedrin,* 68a)

In connection with the need for workers close to the
city to wait for those farther away, so that no one will be

suspected of having worked after the sounding of the *shofar,* it is interesting to cite the following from the *Midrash.* Abba Takhta the Pious was returning to the city when he met a man afflicted with a skin disease, who said to him, "Rabbi, be kind to me, and carry me into the city." Abba said, "If I leave my knapsack here, how shall I support my family? But if I leave this afflicted man here, I shall deserve to be punished." Abba placed moral duty above self-interest, and carried the sick man into the city; and then he returned for his knapsack. When he re-entered the city toward dark, the people exclaimed, "Is this Abba Takhta the Pious?" And he, too, was worried lest he desecrated the Sabbath, but a miracle happened, and God caused the sun to shine. (*Kohelet Rabbah,* 9:7)

A similar miracle is related concerning those who attended Rabbi Yehudah Hanassi's funeral. The Rabbi was buried in Beit Shearim, on Friday.The day was prolonged until the people of the city were able to return home, broil their fish, fill their jugs with water, and light their lamps. Then the sun sat, and the rooster crowed. To calm the people who were worried lest they desecrate the Sabbath, a voice from heaven proclaimed, "All who were present at the funeral have merited eternal life." (*Kohelet Rabbah,* 7:11, 9:10)

35. HULIN, 26b
36. Josephus, WARS OF THE JEWS, IV. 9:12
37. SHABBAT, 9b

Tosafot calls attention to the teaching in *Pesahim* (quoted by us elsewhere) that one may not eat even after *minha,* until after dark, so that he receive the Sabbath while craving food.

38. ERUVIN, 40b
39. SHABBAT, *Mishna,* 1:3
40. *Ibid.,* 119b
41. *Ibid., Mishna,* 2:6
42. ROSH HASHANAH, 9a

From the Torah's teaching ". . . on the ninth, in the evening. . . ." (Lev. 23:32) that we start the fast before sunset, Rabbi Ishmael drew the principle that we take from the non-holy and add to the holy, both at the beginning and at the conclusion of a holy day (*mosiphin miko-desh al khol*).

43. MEKHILTA, *Shabbata*, 2

The *Mekhilta* reasons as follows: Since the Torah teaches, "In plowing and reaping rest" (Exod. 34:21), which implies that one should rest on the eve of the sabbatical year from work needed during the sabbatical year (that is, one must not plow on the eve of the sabbatical year so that he should benefit therefrom during the sabbatical year, when the earth has to lie fallow), we might infer (for both are holy to God, and the Sabbath is even holier) that one is also required to rest on the eve of the Sabbath from work needed during the Sabbath; and hence one should not be permitted to light a lamp, or make a fire which would be enjoyed during the Sabbath. To preclude such possible inference the Torah emphasizes, "Do not kindle a fire *on* the Sabbath" (Exod. 35:3). This implies, that one may not make a fire on the Sabbath, but one may make a fire on the eve of the Sabbath for enjoyment during the Sabbath.

Hayim Leshitz quotes Weiss, in agreement, that the above *Mekhilta* interpretation was directed against the Sadducee view, according to which the enjoyment of fire is forbidden on the Sabbath. Leshitz also refers to the disagreement between the schools of Shammai and Hillel concerning work started before the Sabbath, but which continues during the Sabbath, which Beit Hillel permit and the Beit Shammai forbid. According to the Babylonian Talmud the issue in dispute is the matter of resting one's vessels (*shevitat kelim*), but according to the Yerushalmi the issue is whether one may begin before the Sabbath, work which will be completed after sunset (*Sinai* Magazine Vol. 20, No. 3, p. 161). However, even Beit Shammai permit the enjoyment of a lamp and a fire because, as explained elsewhere, when the lamp is lit and the fire is ignited it is as if their work is already completed.

44. YALKUT SHIMONI, *Beha'alotkha*

45. SHABBAT, 25b

Rashi explains that where there is no light there is no peace, for one has to eat in darkness; and one also stumbles in the dark.

46. *Loc. cit.*
47. *Ibid.,* 23b
48. *Loc. cit.*
48. *Loc. cit.*
50. Rashi, in commenting on the Mishna's teaching that women die at childbirth for negligence of Sabbath candle lighting, says that as a house needs the lighting of candles it is the woman's responsibility. (*Shabbat,* 31b, 32a)

Because "the soul of man (Adam) is the light of God" (Proverbs 20:27), and Eve caused it to go out (by inducing Adam to sin), she was given the *mitzvah* of lighting the Sabbath candles to atone for her sin. (*Yerushalmi, Shabbat,* 2:6). Reference to this is also made in the cited Babylonian Talmud. (See also the *Yalkut Shimoni,* Proverbs, ch. 20, where this is stated very clearly.)

51. SHABBAT, 23b, 34b, 35b
52. SHABBAT, *Mishna,* 2:1, 21a
53. SHABBAT, *Mishna,* 2:4; *Tosephta,* 2:3; 25b

Oils that might cause the lamp to go out are forbidden lest one will try to keep it from becoming extinguished. (Also, one may have to eat his meal without light.)

54. SHABBAT, *Tosephta,* 2:5

Said Rabbi Yehudah, "When we were in Beit Nitze of Lod, we used to perforate a shell of an egg, fill it with oil, and place it on the lamp, in order to prolong its burning." Rabbi Tarphon and the elders were present, and they did not object.

When the potter joined it with mortar it is permissible according to all, for one will not come to take of its oil.

55. MEKHILTA, *Bahodesh,* 7; *Berakhot,* 33a

Women, too, are obligated to fulfill the *mitzvah* of *Kiddush,* according to the Torah. (*Berakhot,* 20b)

Large steps (in walking) impair eyesight; but drinking from the *Kiddush* cup on Sabbath eve will help restore the lost vision. (*Ibid.,* 43b)

56. PESAHIM, 106a
57. *Ibid.,* 97a, b
58. *Ibid.,* 114a; BERAKHOT, *Tosephta,* ch. 5
59. PESAHIM, 117b

The *beit din* (religious court) proclaims the full months and leap years.

60. *Ibid.*, 100a; *BERAKHOT, Tosephta*, ch. 5

According to Rabbi Yose, one may eat until dark. If one started the meal before *minha* and it became dark, he must stop the meal, recite grace and then the *Kiddush;* but according to Rabbi Yose, he need not stop. Once it happened that Rabbi Shimeon ben Gamaliel, Rabbi Yehudah and Rabbi Yose were dining in Acco on Friday afternoon. When it became dark, Rabbi Shimeon said to Rabbi Yose, "Rabbi, shall we stop because of Rabbi Yehudah our colleague?" Rabbi Yose answered, "You always praise my opinion to him, and now you ask me to follow his opinion!" Rabbi Shimeon then said, "In that case let us not stop, lest the students conclude that it is mandatory to stop." However, according to Shmuel the law is neither like Rabbi Yose nor like Rabbi Yehudah, but one covers the food and recites the *Kiddush*. (Pesahim, 99b, 100a)

If it became dark while a group was dining on Friday, a cup of wine is brought, over which one diner recites the *Kiddush* and another the grace, according to Rabbi Yehudah. But according to Rabbi they eat until they finish. Then two cups are brought, one for grace and the second for *Kiddush*. The *Gemara* asks why two cups are necessary. The answer is given by Rabbi Sheshet who de-declared that two *kedushot* (two kinds of holiness) are not recited over one cup, for *mitzvot* must not be treated package-wise, which would make it appear like a burden. (*Ibid.*, 102a)

61. *Ibid.*, 100b

The Gemara tells that Rabbah bar Huna visited the *Reish Galuta* after the synagogue service on Sabbath eve. When he was brought the tray of food, he covered it with a cloth, and recited the *Kiddush*. The *Rashbam* explains that covering the bread was like removing the table with the food. The *Rashbam* then refers to the *Sh'iltot diRabbi Ahai Gaon, Parshat* Yithro, for the full explanation, which is as follows. The tray with food is not brought in before the *Kiddush* but after, in honor of the Sabbath. However, if it was brought in, it is not taken out but covered, while the *Kiddush* is recited, in accordance with the *Baraita,* which states, "And they agree that the table (with food) is not brought in until after the *Kiddush*. If it was brought in, it is covered with a cloth." For this reason, the *Rashbam* concludes, it is customary to cover the bread until after the *Kiddush,* on Sabbath and festivals. (*Loc. cit.*)

Tosaphot comments as follows: They used to supply each diner with a small table. These tables were removed at the end of the meal, except the table of the one who led in grace. The tables were brought in after the recitation of the *Kiddush*. . . . Today, when our tables are big, and it would be difficult to bring them in after the recitation of the *Kiddush* . . . we cover (the bread) with a cloth, and recite the *Kiddush*. The reason is given in the *Sh'iltot*. Others say that it is in remembrance of the *manna,* which did not come down on the Sabbath, and which was sandwiched in between two layers of dew. What the Gemara in *Shabbat* means when it states that "if the angels find the table set" is that the table was set elsewhere, and brought in after the *Kiddush,* to the place where the meal was to be eaten. (*Loc. cit.*)

62. MEKHILTA, *Vayassa,* 5; *Shabbat,* 117a

The *Mekhilta* deduces that there should be three meals on the Sabbath, from the three "today's" in the verse, "And Moses said, 'Eat it today, because today is Sabbath to the Lord; today you will not find it in the field'" (Exod. 16:25).

63. BABA BATRA, 9a

64. HULIN, 111a

Rabba bar Rabbi Huna visited Rabba bar Rabbi Nahman on a Sabbath. The guest asked, when an abundant quantity of white bread covered with honey and oil, was served, "Did you know I was coming?" He was answered, "Are you more important than she, concerning whom it says, 'And you shall call the Sabbath a delight?'" (Is. 58:13).

65. SHABBAT, 118b, 119a

Garlic is conducive to fertility (according to talmudic belief), and fish symbolizes it. (*Berakhot,* 20a, 40a; *Baba Kama,* 82a; *Gen.,* 48:16) Why are Babylonian (Jewish)

festivals joyous? asks the Talmud; and answers, Because
they (the Jews of Babylonia) are poor (and have better
food on the Sabbath). (*Shabbat*, 145a) However, for the
poor this was not an unmixed good, as is evident from the
following question and answer. "All the days of the poor
are unhappy" (Prov. 15:15): Asked Rabbi Yehoshua ben
Levi, "Are there not the Sabbath and festivals?" "This is
in accordance with Shmuel's teaching: 'A change in eating routine causes stomach trouble.'" (*Gitin*, 101a)

66. SHABBAT, 119a

Eagerness to make the Sabbath meal as palatable as
possible, in due time produced the desired results, with
approval by non-Jews, as is seen in the following incidents
related in the Talmud. A Roman asked Rabbi Yeshoshua
ben Hanania, "Why is the Sabbath broth fragrant?" The
Rabbi answered, "We have a spice named *Shabbat*, which
makes the broth fragrant." The Roman then said, "Give
me some of the spice." Rabbi Yehoshua answered, "It works
only for those who keep the Sabbath." (The love and per-
sistence with which the meal is prepared in honor of the
Sabbath cannot be transferred to one who tries to imitate
it casually.) (*Shabbat*, 119a)

Rabbi Yehudah Hanassi prepared a cold meal for the
Emperor Antoninus on the Sabbath, and once on a weekday he prepared a hot meal. Antoninus said, "I enjoyed
the cold meal more." Rabbi answered, "The hot one lacked
a spice." Antoninus said, "What spice can be lacking
in the Emperor's storehouse?" (where Rabbi Yehudah
obtained the ingredients). Rabbi answered, "*Shabbat*. Do
you have the *Shabbat*?" (*Loc. cit.*)

On the Sabbath and festivals, states the Talmud, a man
bases his meal on wine. (*Berakhot*, 42b)

67. MEKHILTA, *Kaspa*, 3

This is inferred from the command that ". . . your ox
and donkey may rest." (Exod. 23:12). If the animal is
locked up and not allowed to graze, says the *Mekhilta*, it
is not resting; but suffering.

68. MINAHOT, 43b

69. SHABBAT, 113a; PESIKTA, 23:6

Rashi explains that lowering the garments makes one

appear like the wealthy who do not have to raise their garments, to keep them from being in the way during their work.

When Rabbi Simlai once taught (as Rabbi Hanan) that one should sanctify the Sabbath also with having a special garment for the Sabbath, his students burst into tears, and they sobbed, "We have to wear on the Sabbath what we wear on weekdays." He said to them, "Nevertheless, try to make some change." (*Yerushalmi, Peah,* ch. 8; *Pesikta,* 23:1)

70. YERUSHALMI, *Shabbat,* 15:3; *Pesikta,* 23:9; DEUTERONOMY RABBAH, 3

Our summary is based on these typical rabbinic views: "Do you think that I (God) gave you the Sabbath as a burden? I gave it to you for your benefit." How? Explained Rabbi Hiyya bar Abba, "Keep the Sabbath holy with food, drink and clean garments, enjoy yourself, and I shall reward you."

According to Rabbi Hiyya, the Sabbath was given only for joy. But according to Rabbi Shmuel bar Nahman "the Sabbath was given only for the teaching of Torah." In the Yerushalmi we find that Rabbi Shmuel, too, believes that the Sabbath was given for eating and drinking, but since man sins with his mouth, he was permitted to study the Torah. The conclusion is that the two rabbis are in basic agreement that the Sabbath be used for physical enjoyment *and* for study, and that laborers should devote themselves (more) to study, whereas scholars "who toil the entire week over their studies" should on the Sabbath enjoy themselves (more) with physical pleasures.

According to Rabbi Yehoshua of Sokhnin, the enjoyment of the Sabbath is a *mitzvah* meriting God's fulfilment of one's pleas.

Philo reflects the rabbinic view in the following passage: "The Torah forbids work, to lighten from man his ceaseless labor, and to refresh him. Physical labor is forbidden, but not intellectual pursuits. One should occupy himself with philosophical study, for mental and spiritual perfection. . . . One sees that Moses does not allow the followers of the Torah to be idle even a moment. On the contrary,

since we are made up of body and soul, he (Moses) allots
to each its necessary share, at the appropriate time." (*Sefer
HaShabbat*, pp. 14-17)

71. KETUBOT, 62b

That the Sabbath should not be observed as a solemn
day in which one must abstain from all physical pleasures,
the *Sifra* infers from the Torah's designating the Day of
Atonement as an exclusively solemn day, for the Torah
says, "It is a solemn rest to you" (Lev. 16:31), implying
that only *it* (Yom Kippur) is a solemn day on which all
the physical pleasures are forbidden. (*Sifra, Aharei Mot*)

72. BABA KAMA, 82a

This may also be the reason for eating fish, the symbol
of fruitfulness, on Friday evening. *Jubilees* (ch. 50), however, forbids cohabitation on the Sabbath. R. H. Charles
explains: "This law probably sprang from the fanatical
period referred to in *Sanhedrin* (46a), the period of Syro-
Greek domination."

73. MEKHILTA, *Bahodesh, 7*

The inference is from the Torah's declaration, "Six days
labor and do all your work" (Exod. 20:). The *Mekhilta*
asks, "Is it possible for a person to do all his work in six
days?" The answer is: "Rest as if all your work were done."

74. SHABBAT, 12a, 113a, 150a

From the verse, "And honor it by keeping from the
pursuit of your business. . . ." (Is. 58:13), the Talmud
draws this teaching: "Your Sabbath garments must not be
like your weekday garments; your walking on the Sabbath
must not be like your walking on weekdays. *Your* needs
are forbidden, but *community* needs are permitted. (But)
your talk on the Sabbath should not be like your talk on
weekdays."

Although it is forbidden to pray for one's needs on the
Sabbath, the words, "Our Shepherd, feed, sustain . . . us"
are retained in the grace because they are part of the grace
pattern and their recitation does not cause any worry.
(*Yerushalmi, Shabbat*, ch. 15; *Lev. Rabbah*, 34:16)

In connection with the prohibition against visiting
one's field on the Sabbath, Rabbi Berakhia told that once
a *hassid* went, on the Sabbath, to see what his vineyard

5

needed. He found that it needed fencing of a breach. Upon reconsidering that he thought about it on the Sabbath, he decided never to put up the fence. (*Pesikta*, 23:3; *Lev. Rabbah*, 34:16)

Where a person was buried on Friday toward dark in a cemetery near a city, the seven *maamadot* and *moshavot* (the stopping and sitting down on the way home from the cemetery, in order to console the mourners) are permissible even after the Sabbath has already started. (*Baba Batra*, 100b)

75. BABA BATRA, 91a

This is permissible only in connection with the price drop of fine garments, which are purchased only by the well-to-do who can afford higher prices. But the congregation may not pray for a rise in price of such garments as are purchased by the poor. (*Rashbam* commentary.)

76. BERAKHOT, 18a; MOED KATAN, 23a

77. YERUSHALMI, *Berakhot*, 2:7; *Moed Katan*, 3:5

The Yerushalmi relates that Rabbi Yose bar Halaphta had praised Rabbi Meir as a great man. However, when Rabbi Meir greeted mourners on the Sabbath, the people of Sepphoris were surprised, and questioned Rabbi Yose's opinion, until Rabbi Yose explained to them that Rabbi Meir purposely greeted the mourners to indicate that there is no mourning on the Sabbath. According to a Midrash, Rabbi Meir's family practiced the teaching even when they were personally stricken. For Rabbi Meir's two chidren died on the Sabbath, while he was in the *beit hamidrash*. Returning home at night, he inquired about the whereabouts of the children (not having been told what happened). Beruriah asked him to recite the *havdallah* first, and then she gently revealed the tragic truth. (*Yalkut Shimoni, Proverbs,* 31)

78. TAANIT, 26b

79. NEDARIM, 25b, 66a

The Book of Judith (8:6) tells us that the heroine fasted during her widowhood except on Sabbath, festivals, new moon and the days on the eve of these holy days. Fasting on the Sabbath necessitates another fast, in atonement. (*Berakhot*, 31b)

80. ERUVIN, 96a MINAHOT, 36b; YERUSHALMI, *Shabbat*, 13:3; TANHUMA, *Va-yikra*

The *Sifra,* commenting on the verse, "My Sabbaths keep, and be in awe of My sanctuary, I am the Lord" (Lev. 19:31), declares that one should be in awe not of the Sabbath but of Him Who commanded it; that is, the Sabbath has only delegated holiness. (The *Sifra* teaching may also be directed against the pagan belief that certain days were unlucky.)

82. YERUSHALMI, *Beitza,* 5:2

83. ERUVIN, 104a

Because the Sabbath is a day of complete rest, which is not to be disturbed by dispensable noise, one must not put wheat into a water mill on Friday, unless it can be ground before the Sabbath, even according to Beit Hillel who reject Beit Shammai's view that the Torah requires that a man's vessels, too, rest. (*Shabbat,* 18a)

84. YERUSHALMI, *Shabbat,* 15:3

From the verse, "It is Sabbath to the Lord," Rabbi Tanhuma infers, "Rest like your God. He rested from speech. You, too, rest from speech."

85. PESAHIM, 50b

86. NEDARIM, 37b

87. MEKHILTA, *Bahodesh,* 7

A somewhat different, abridged and interpretative version of the *Mekhilta* discussion is found in the *Pesikta*. It follows: The School of Rabbi Ismael taught: He blessed it with *manna,* and sanctified it with *manna.* Every day only one *omer* was gathered, but for the Sabbath two *omrim* were gathered. Rabbi Nathan taught: He sanctified it with a blessing. From this the rabbis inferred that the holiness of the day is proclaimed over wine at the inception of the Sabbath. Rabbi said: He sanctified it with dress (in honor of the Sabbath). (*Pesikta,* 23:6)

88. SHEVUOT, 18b

Said Rabbi Yohanan, He who recites the *havdallah* over wine will have male children.

89. BERAKHOT, 33b, 51b, 52b

Rashi explains that although, as the Gemara states, Ezra and the Men of the Great Assembly instituted blessings, prayers, *Kiddush* and *havdallah,* the Schools of Hillel and Shammai dispute the sequence of the blessings because the sequence of the original instituted arrangement (*tekanah*) was forgotten—in the changes from the original recitation of the *havdallah* in the *Amidah* to the one over the wine (when the people prospered), to the one in the *Amidah* again (when they became poor again). (*Berakhot*, 33a)

90. PESAHIM, 103a
91. *Loc. cit.*
92. BERAKHOT, 53a

Although the Gemara (*Minahot*, 35b; *Pesahim,* 7b, 119b, etc.) states that a blessing must precede the enjoyment of something or the performance of a *mitzvah,* in the case of the *havdallah* light, the blessing follows the enjoyment, necessarily. For elsewhere, one sees the thing to be enjoyed, but light is enjoyed as soon as one sees it.

93. BERAKHOT, *Tosephta,* ch. 5, 53a

In order to keep from wasting time, the students of Rabban Gamaliel did not say *Marpe* ('Gesundheit') when one sneezed during the studies.

94. BERAKHOT, 54a; GEN. RABBAH, 11:12
95. PESAHIM, 104a
96. *Ibid.,* 105b
97. *Ibid.,* 106a
98. SHABBAT, 150b
99. *Ibid.,* 119b
100. SHABBAT, 151a

CHAPTER IX

1. One rabbi specifically equates the public desecration of the Sabbath with idolatry. Therefore, he teaches that sacrifices may be accepted from habitual Jewish sinners (*poshei Yisrael*) in order to encourage them to repent, except from those who practice idolatry and who desecrate the Sabbath publicly. (*Eruvin,* 69b)

The Torah also decrees death for several types of disobedience, involving the rebellious son (*ben sorer umoreh*), a rebellious member of the *Sanhedrin* (*zaken mamre*) and a false prophet (*n'vi hasheker*), all under extremely limited circumstances. Probably all transgress within the category of idolatry, for they all rebelliously challenge traditional authority seeking to fulfill God's will.

2. In the absence of qualified witnesses and adequate warning, a transgressor is subject only to "death by heaven" (*mitah biyedei shamayim*) commonly associated with the sentence expressed by the Torah in the words, "and the soul shall be cut off from her people" (also referred to as *karet*). However, the concrete punishment may have been ostracism from the community. It is probably to such cases that the author of the *Zadokite Fragments* refers when he states that "he who strays and desecrates the Sabbath, shall not be put to death, but it shall be the duty of the sons of men to watch him; and should he be healed of it, they shall continue to watch him for seven years, and then he shall be readmitted to the congregation." (*Fragments of a Zadokite Work*, ch. 14)

3. MEKHILTA, *Shabbata*, 1

4. SIFREI, *Sh'lah L'kha; Baba Batra*, 119a

   The *Sifrei*, commenting on the verse, "They found a man. . . ." (Num. 15:32-36) states: Moses appointed guards who discovered and warned the wood gatherer concerning the category of work (transgressed by him). . . . All who are subject to the penalty of *karet* are imprisoned.

   The *Mekhilta* deduces the need of warnings against day and night transgressions as follows: "And the seventh day is a sabbath to the Lord your God. Do not do any kind of work on it" (Exod. 31:14-17) constitutes the warning (for day and night); "who ever will work on it shall be put to death" is the penalty. (*Mekhilta, Bahodesh*, 7)

   The *Mekhilta's* need to single out night desecration may be directed against some sectarian view.

5. SANHEDRIN, 8b

   One who works at the end of Yom Kippur which is on a Sabbath eve is therefore not subject to the death penalty, for since it is uncertain whether he desecrated Yom Kippur or the Sabbath (the two having different penalties), he cannot be warned definitely. (*Mekhilta, Shabbata*, 2) However, one who works on Yom Kippur coming on a Sabbath does

incur the death penalty (for it is no worse than working on a plain Sabbath). (*Sifra, Emor*)
6. YEVAMOT, 90b; SANHEDRIN, 46b

Thus, the Talmud relates, a man who rode on a horse during the Sabbath, in the period of (Syrian) Greek religious persecution, was sentenced to be stoned, not because he deserved the penalty but because the *times* necessitated it.
7. SHABBAT, 70a

The rabbinic reluctance to decree the death penalty should be contrasted with the sectarian severity as reflected in the following *Jubilees* excerpts: "Only sacrifices may be offered on the Sabbath in God's sanctuary, to atone for Israel. . . . But every man who will work or kindle a fire or carry a load on his animal or sail in a boat on the sea, or who strikes and kills anyone or slaughters an animal or bird or fasts (or, perhaps, hunts, *tzad*, instead of *tzam*, meaning fasts) or wars on the Sabbath . . . shall die. . . . The man who will lie with a woman, and who will discuss work to be done that day . . . or have dealings, or will draw water, which he did not prepare on the sixth day, and who carries a load from his tent or house shall die." (*Jubilees*, ch. 50) Of course, the above could have been written during the period of religious persecution referred to in note 6.

One rabbi contended that there is no physical punishment for transgressing the *t'hum Shabbat*, as appears from the following dispute in the *Yerushalmi*: Rabbi Shimeon bar Yosi bar Lekunia said, "One is lashed, according to the Torah, if he transgresses the law of *t'hum Shabbat*." Rabbi Hiyya asked, "Is not the Torah punishment for desecration of the Sabbath stoning or *karet*?" Rabbi Shimeon answered that the verse, "Let no one go out of his place on the seventh day" (Exod. 16:29), interpreted to apply to one who moves beyond the 2000 cubit allowed from one's residence or city, is a *lav* (a 'do not' command, for the transgression of which one is lashed). Rabbi Hiyya retorted that this verse is not like the usual *lav* transgressions, for unlike them it does not begin with the word *lo*, but with *al*. The Talmud concludes that the two rabbis persisted in their opinions—and according to Rabbi Hiyya the transgression does not entail lashing. (*Yerushalmi, Pesahim*, 6:1)

9. SANHEDRIN, 8b
10. SANHEDRIN, 35a
11. BABA KAMA, 54b, 87a
    The reason is that where a person incurs two kinds of penalties, he is given only one, the more severe one *(kam leih bid'rabel minei)*.
12. SHABBAT, *Tosephta*, 9:3
13. SIFRA, *Va-yikra* (Lev. 4:22-23); SHABBAT, *Mishna*, 8:1
    In the *Yerushalmi* we find this simple explanation: "Why is it," asks Rabbi Yose, "that if one knows that today is Sabbath but not that the kinds of work are forbidden, he is *hayav* for each category of work? Because if the would-be transgressor were told that a specific type of work is forbidden he would nevertheless do the others about which he remains unreminded. Why is it that one who forgets that it is Sabbath, but knows that the kinds of work are forbidden, brings only one sacrifice for all types of work done? Because if he were told that it is Sabbath, he would refrain from all transgressions." *(Yerushalmi, Shabbat, 7:1)*
    He who commits two different *avot* or *toldot* of labor brings two sacrifices, but he offers only one sacrifice for all transgressions within one category. *(Baba Kama, 2a)*
14. SHABBAT, *Mishna*, 11:6
15. SHABBAT, *Tosephta*, 9:3
16. SHABBAT, *Mishna*, 2:6
17. MEKHILTA, *Vayassa*, 6
18. *Ibid., Shabbata*, 1
19. SIFRA, *Aharei Mot*
    This may have been taught during a time of religious persecution.
20. JUBILEES, ch. 2
21. EXODUS RABBAH, 25:12; SHABBAT, 118b, where the number is *two* Sabbaths.
22. MEKHILTA, *Vayassa*, 5

CHAPTER X

1. MEKHILTA, *Bahodesh*, 8
2. BABA KAMA, 15a
3. BERAKHOT, 20b

The Mishna in *Kedushin* lays down the rule that both men and women must keep all 'do not' *(lo taaseh)* commands; both must fulfil the 'do commands' *(aseh)* which apply throughout the day and the year; but positive commands which are performed only periodically *(mitzvot aseh she'hazman g'rama)* only men are obligated to keep. The Gemara shows that this rule has exceptions, for women are also required to eat *matza* on the first night of Passover, to rejoice on festivals, etc. although these *mitzvot* are seasonal; and study of the Torah, raising a family, etc. are not incumbent on women although they apply at all times. *(Kedushin, 29a, 34a)*

4. MEKHILTA, *Bahodesh,* 7
5. YEVAMOT, 113b; SHABBAT, *Mishna,* 16:6
6. MEKHILTA, *Shabbata,* 1
7. *Ibid., Bahodesh,* 7
8. *Ibid., Kaspa,* 3; KREITUT, 9a
9. SHABBAT, 19a
10. AVODAH ZARA, 15a

Dr. Louis Ginzberg thinks this reason far-fetched. The real reason, he writes, is economic, to protect the Jewish Palestinian settlement, and he cites the *Yerushalmi (Pesahim,* 4:3) in support of his view. (Ginzberg, *Of Jewish law and Lore,* pp. 83-84, 246) However, the reason given in *Avodah Zara* is similar to the one given in ch. 14 of *Zadokite Fragments—* a very early document, according to some scholars. There it decrees, "Let no man sell clean animals and fowl to the heathens, so that they should not sacrifice them." Also, even from the Yerushalmi it seems that the reason given in *Avodah Zara* was regarded valid.

11. SHABBAT, *Tosephta,* 14:10
12. SHABBAT, 18b
13. DEUTERONOMY RABBAH, 1:21; *SHABBAT,* 153a
14. SHABBAT, *Tosephta,* 14:9; 121a; YERUSHALMI, *Nedarim,* ch. 4

Nevertheless, the pious did tell the non-Jew to desist, as is seen from the following two incidents related in the Talmud. Once, when a fire broke out in the yard of Yoseph ben Simai of Sihim, the governor of Sepphoris sent firemen to extinguish the fire, but Yoseph told them to desist (because of the Sabbath). According to the Tosephta, the fire was miraculously put out by rain. At the end of the Sabbath, Yoseph paid all firemen as if they had performed their service.

Rabbi Yonah, too, did not allow his neighbors to put out a fire on his property; and he promised to pay for all damages to neighbors' property, but by a miracle there was no damage.

15. SHABBAT, *Tosephta,* 14:11

CHAPTER XI

1. MEKHILTA, *Shabbata,* 1
2. ESTHER RABBAH, 7
3. RUTH RABBAH, 3
4. PESIKTA, 23:6-7; SHABBAT, 119a
5. BABA METZIA, *Mishna,* ch. 4 (pp. 51b, 52a)
6. MEGILLAH, 27b
7. TAANIT, 24a
8. *Ibid.,* 25a
9. GEN. RABBAH, 11:4
10. PESIKTA, 23:6-7; *SHABBAT,* 119a
    "According to some versions, the 'hassid' bought the fish for the eve of a precious day, on which we are freed from all sins." This could apply also to the Sabbath, for according to Philo the Sabbath is a day for spiritual self-analysis. More likely, the pious man brought his special food for all holy days.
11. YERUSHALMI, *Haggiga,* 2:1
12. YERUSHALMI, *Taanit,* 4; *Lamentations Rabbah* (quoted in SEFER HASHABBAT, p. 26)
13. GITIN, 38b
14. SHABBAT, 40a
14. GITIN, 53b
16. SHABBAT, 38a
17. Philo, PHILOSOPHICAL WRITINGS, p. 40
18. EXODUS RABBAH, 25:11; DEUTERONOMY RABBAH, 1:21; SANHEDRIN, 58b, 59a
    "Merits death" must be taken in the sense that the Mishna speaks of those who idle from their studies as

endangering their lives (*Avot,* 3:5, 9, 10). Maimonides in his *Mishnah Torah* (chapter 10 of *Laws of Kings and Wars*) explains that the heathen is told that he merits death—but is not given the punishment, because he innovates a religion. He must either become a full convert or adhere to his own religion. The former point is also suggested by the *Yalkut Shimoni,* who quotes *Deuteronomy Rabbah* in these words: "Said Rabbi Yose bar Rabbi Hanina, a heathen who keeps the Sabbath before he accepted circumcision merits death. Why? Because he was not commanded it, and does not observe it properly." Then he goes on and quotes the passage about the king and the matron. (*Yalkut Shimoni, Exod,* 31:391)

It seems to us in all humility, that the discussion in *Sanhedrin* tends to bear out the approach of Maimonides. Reish Lakish bases the prohibition of a heathen to rest, on Genesis 8:22; i.e., a heathen who rests merely idles. Rabina, a rabbi of the fifth century, explains that this also applies to one who rests on Monday, but he does not say "even on Sunday."

A word must also be said about the analogy with the stranger who intrudes while the king and the noblewoman carry on their dialogue. The Sabbath is not a mere day of rest, but one dedicated to God. The Sabbath testifies that God created the world, and no one else but He must be worshipped. To remain a heathen (i.e., not to accept circumcision, the symbol of the covenant between God and Abraham, and thus become one who acknowledges Him) while one accepts the Sabbath, is to endanger the entire basic philosophy of the Sabbath.

19. SIFRA, *Behar* (Lev. 26:2)
20. SHABBAT, 69b

CHAPTER XII

1. The famous rabbinic teaching concerning a heathen who rests on the Sabbath (quoted in the preceding chapter) may have been aimed not only against the dilution of the traditional Sabbath but also against irritating the Christians. The Talmud's statement (although made by a fifth century

Babylonian Amora) that even if one rests on Monday (but not mentioning Sunday) seems to bear out this view. (*Sanhedrin*, 58b) In *Taanit* (27b) Rabbi Yohanan says specifically that the men of the stations (*anshei ma'amadot*) did not fast on Sunday because of the Christians (who would be angry, as explained—rightly we believe—by Gersonides).

2. Philo, PHILOSOPHICAL WRITINGS, p. 103
3. Josephus, AGAINST APION, quoted in *Sabbath, Day of Delight*, p. 128
4. II MACCABEES, 15

An extreme example of self-sacrifice in behalf of the Sabbath is the episode of the *Hassidim* who refused even to camouflage their hiding place in the cave, because that necessitated the lifting of stones which may not be handled on the Sabbath. (i *Maccabees*, 1-2)

As mentioned in an earlier chapter, the Maccabees ruled that for self-defense, dispensation of the Sabbath is permissible. However, the ruling did not become known immediately among non-Jews, for the attacking pagans seemed surprised when Jews fought in self-defense on the Sabbath, as in the cases of Jonathan versus Bacchides (*Antiquities*, XIII:1) and Asineus and Anileus, who led the Jewish rebellion in Partia (*Antiquities*, XVIII:9).

The unhappy role of apostates in the attempt to suppress Jewish observance of the Sabbath is recorded both by Josephus and the Talmud. The former relates that the ethnarch of the Jews in Antioch turned against the people and prevented them from resting on the Sabbath. (Josephus, *Wars*, VII, 3:3) The Yerushalmi relates that once, in time of religious persecution, the Jews would have found a way of evading forced desecration of the Sabbath if not for the apostate Elisha ben Abuya. The burdens in public domains were carried by two persons simultaneously, or the burden was unloaded in a *carmelit*, there being in neither case a desecration of Torah law. Elisha ben Abuya called this maneuver to the attention of the persecutors. He urged them to compel individual Jews to carry burdens, without being permitted to stop in a *carmelit*. (*Yerushalmi*, *Hagiah*, 2:1)

An example of individual pagan hostility to the Sabbath

is the following (accepted by some rabbis as sufficiently valid for declaring the wife of the reported victim a widow) : A heathen said to a Jew, on the Sabbath, "Pluck some vegetables for my cattle, or I shall kill you as I killed that Jew who disobeyed me when I ordered him to cook for me on the Sabbath." (*Yevamot,* 121b)
5. Salo Baron, A SOCIAL AND RELIGIOUS HISTORY OF THE JEWS, Vol. I, p. 192
6. Quoted by Isaac Schwab, THE SABBATH IN HISTORY, p. 58
7. LAMENTATIONS RABBAH
   Pagans ridiculed alleged Jewish non-observance as well as observance. Thus, the Talmud relates that a Jew and a heathen were once sitting in a boat laden with barrels of wine, on a Friday. When the *shofar,* proclaiming the arrival of the Sabbath, sounded, the Jew left. Since the Jew was unable to return to the boat on Sabbath, the question arose whether the wine, left with the heathen, was kosher. Rava ruled that it was, for the heathen did not know definitely that the Jew would not return. Rava supports his opinion by quoting Eisur the convert, who said, "When we were still heathens we used to say that Jews do not keep the Sabbath, for if they did, many purses would be found in the *shuk* (on Friday eve, thrown away by delayed persons rushing home)." (*Avodah Zara* 70a)
   According to Salo Baron, ridicule of the Jewish Sabbath co-existed with tolerance of Jewish rights. He writes. "Even in litigations of Jews against non-Jews, and in which state courts were to administer justice, the Jews enjoyed, since the days of Augustus, the privilege of not being cited as parties or witnesses on a Sabbath. At the same time, Roman public opinion often viewed the Sabbath as simply an expression of Jewish laziness." (Salo Baron, *The Jewish Community,* Vol. I, p. 110)
   Josephus himself (a prejudiced witness!) deplored taking advantage of the pagan respect for the Jewish Sabbath. He relates that John (one of the leaders in the war with Rome) told Titus that he (John) could not discuss the issues of war and peace on the Sabbath, for "even the Romans were not ignorant how the period of the seventh day was among

them (the Jews) a cessation from all labors; and that he who should compel them to transgress the law about that day would be equally guilty with those who were compelled to transgress it." "Thus," comments Josephus, "did this man put a trick upon Titus, not so much out of regard to the seventh day, as to his own preservation." (Josephus, *Wars*, IV. 2:3)

9. MEGILLAH, 17a
10. ROSH HASHANAH, 19a; TAANIT, 18a; ESTHER RAB-BAH, 7
11. MATTHEW, 12:1-3; MARK, 2:23-38; LUKE 6:1-10
12. LUKE, 13-10-17

To counteract this Christian belief that the Sabbath law could be abrogated, the *Mekhilta* stresses, "See that the Lord gives you the Sabbath" (Exod. 16:29). Moses said, "Be careful to observe it, for God gives it to you." (*Mekhilta, Vayassa*, 6)

13. JOHN, 5:5-19
14. Salo Baron, HISTORY OF THE JEWS, VOL. II, ch. 12, note 6
    See also note 1 to this chapter.
15. GENESIS RABBAH, 11
16. The Midrash, basing its reason on the verse, "See that the Lord has given you the Sabbath" (Exod. 16:29), gives a more traditional answer. "Why not, *know*, but, *see?*" asks the Midrash. "God said," it answers, "if the heathens should ask you, 'Why do you keep the Sabbath on the seventh day?' tell them, see that the *manna* does not come down on the Sabbath." (*Exodus Rabbah*, 25:11)
17. PESIKTA, 23:8
    Obviously this is the answer to the New Testament claim that Jesus could work on the Sabbath like God.
18. Salo Baron, THE JEWISH COMMUNITY, Vol. I, p. 112; HISTORY OF THE JEWS, Vol. II, pp. 188, 134
19. MEKHILTA, *Shabbata*, 1
20. PESIKTA, 23:1
    This probably means that all should remember that God created the world, and that the Jews should keep the Sabbath *mitzvot*.
    See also note 1 to this chapter.

BIBLIOGRAPHY

BIBLIOGRAPHY

MIKRAOT G'DOLOT and Commentaries, *Rashi, Ibn Ezra, Rashbam, Ramban (Nahmanides), S'forno, Or Hahayim, Radak,* and an article by Rabbi Menahem N. Kasher, Shulsinger Brothers, N. Y., 1950.

MEKHILTA de-Rabbi Ishmael, Dr. Jacob Z. Lauterbach, Editor, Jewish Publication Society of America, Philadelphia, 1933.

SIFRA.

SIFREI on *Numbers* and *Deuteronomy* (All three in the MIKRAOT G'DOLOT Edition).

MIDRASH RABBAH, *The Torah and Five Megillot,* Rom, Vilna, 1887.

PESIKTA RABBATI, Warsaw, 1912.

YALKUT SHIMONI, Pardes, N. Y., 1944.

MIDRASH HAGADOL, *B'reishit,* Mosad Harav Kook, Jerusalem, 1947.

TORAH SHELEMAH, Vol. IX, Rabbi M. M. Kasher, New York, 1944.

FROM ADAM TO NOAH (Hebrew), Prof. U. Cassuto, Hebrew University Press, Jerusalem, 1953.

A COMMENTARY ON THE BOOKS OF EXODUS (Hebrew), U. Cassuto, Heb. U. Press, 1953.

A COMMENTARY ON AMOS AND HOSEA, William Rainey Harper, Charles Scribner's Sons, New York, 1915.

THE BOOK OF HUMAN DESTINY, Vol. I, Solomon Goldman, Harper, New York, 1948.

THE BOOK OF HUMAN DESTINY, Vol. II, Solomon Goldman, Jewish Publication Society, Philadelphia, 1949.

A CRITICAL COMMENTARY ON GENESIS, John Skinner, Charles Scribner's Sons, New York, 1925.

BOOK OF JUBILEES, The Apocrypha (Hebrew), Abraham Kahana, Editor, Vol. I, Tel Aviv, 1936.

I MACCABEES, (King James Version).

FRAGMENTS OF A ZADOKITE WORK, The Apocrypha, Vol. II, R. H. Charles, Ed., Oxford, 1913.

BEN SIRA (Ecclesiasticus, Hebrew), B. Kohan, Berlin, 1927.

EDAH V'EDUT (Hebrew), A. M. Haberman, Jerusalem, 1952.

MISHNAYOT and Commentaries, *R. Obadiah mi Bertnura, Tiferet Israel and Tosafot Yom Tov,* Rom, Vilna, 1891.

SEDER MOED, with Commentary by Hanokh Albeck, Mosad Bialik, Jerusalem, 1954.

TOSEPHTA and Commentaries, *Minhat Bikkurim,* etc., Rom, Vilna, 1896.

THE MISHNAH TRANSLATION, Herbert Danby, Oxford University Press, London, 1933.

TALMUD BAVLI and Commentaries, *Rashi, Rashbam, Rabbenu Hananel, Rabbenu Gershom, Maharsha, Shitah M'Kubetzat,* Rom, Vilna, 1908.

TALMUD YERUSHALMI and Commentaries, *Korban Edah,* etc., Gilead Press, New York, 1949.

A DICTIONARY OF THE TALMUD, ETC., Marcus Jastrow, Pardes Publishing House, New York, 1950.

SEFER HA'AGGADAH, Bialik and Ravnitzki, Dvir, 1936.

ABOT D' R. NATHAN (in *Talmud Bavli* Edition).

INTRODUCTION TO THE TALMUD, M. Mielziner, Bloch, N. Y., 1925.

THE WORKS OF JOSEPHUS, The World Syndicate Publishing Co., Cleveland, Ohio.

PHILO, Philosophical Writings, Dr. Hans. Lewy, Editor, East and West Library, 1946.

PHILO, Harry Wolfson, Harvard University Press, 1947.

THE FOUR GOSPELS.

SEFER HASHABBAT, L. Bruch, Ed., Tel Aviv, 1936.

THE PHARISEES, R. Travers Herford, McMillan, N. Y., 1924.

JUDAISM, Vol. II, George F. Moore, Harvard U. Press, 1922.

A SOCIAL AND RELIGIOUS HISTORY OF THE JEWS, Salo Baron, Columbia U. Press, 1953.

THE JEWISH COMMUNITY, Salo Baron, The Jewish Publication Society, Phil., 1942.

ENCYCLOPEDIA OF RELIGION AND ETHICS, Vol. X, James Hastings, Ed.

DOR, DOR V'DORSHOV, Isaac Hirsh Weiss, Berlin, 1924.

THE JEWS: THEIR HISTORY, CULTURE AND RELI-
GION, Vol. I, Dr. Louis Finkelstein, Ed., JPS, 1949.

THE ARCHAOLOGY OF PALESTINE, Dr. William Albright, Penguin Book, 1949.

EXILE AND REDEMPTION in the Literature of Israel
(Hebrew), Dr. Meyer Waxman, Ogen, N. Y., 1952.

THE SABBATH IN HISTORY, Dr. Isaac Schwab, St. Joseph,
Mo., 1888.

SABBATH, *Day of Delight*, Abraham E. Millgram, J.P.S.,
1952.

ON JEWISH LAW AND LORE, Prof. Louis Ginzberg, JPS,
1955.

THE PHARISEES, Louis Finkelstein, JPS, 1946.

RABBINIC ESSAYS, Jacob Z. Lauterbach, Hebrew U. College Press, Cincinnati, 1951.

RABBINICAL ASSEMBLY PROCEEDINGS, 1950.

HASHABBAT, HAAM V'HAARETZ, Zeev Aryeh Rabbiner,
Tel Aviv, 1948.

TOLDOT ISRAEL, Vol. III, Zeev Yaavetz, Ahiever, Jerusalem, 1928.

DIVRE YEME AM OLAM, Vol. II, Simon Dubnow, Tel
Aviv, 1936.

JUDAISM (First Series), Solomon Schechter, JPA, 1938.

MORE NEVUKHIM, Part 2, Chap. 31, R. Moses ben
Maimon.

FAITH FOR FALLIBLES, Nathan A. Barack, Bloch Publishing Co., New York, 1952.

THE JEWISH ENCYCLOPEDIA, Vol. X (pp. 587-605),
Funk and Wagnall, New York, 1905.

OTZAR YISRAEL, J. D. Eisenstein, Vol. X (pp. 42-51),
Pardes Publishing House, New York, 1951.

OTZAR MAAMARE HAZAL, J. D. Eisenstein, Wolf Sales,
New York, 1947.

THE JEWISH QUARTERLY REVIEW, Vol. 36, No. 4
(April, 1946): Vol. 41, No. 4 (April, 1951); Vol. 44, No. 3
(Jan., 1954).

SINAI MAGAZINE (Hebrew), Vol. 20, No. 3 (Sivan, 5717),
Mosad HaRav Kook.

HADOAR Magazine (Hebrew), 30 Shevat, 5717.

MISHNAH TORAH, *Sefer Shoftim, Rambam,* Mosad Harav Kuk, Israel.

YESODOT HATEFILLAH, Eliezer Levi, Abraham Zion Pub. House, Israel.

TOLDOT HAEMUNAH HAYISRAELIT (Vols. I, IV) Yehezkel Kaufmann, Mosad Bialik, Israel, 1937, 1956.

THE RELIGION OF ISRAEL, Yehezkel Kaufmann (Translated and Abridged by Moshe Greenberg), The University of Chicago Press, Chicago, Ill., 1960.

THE LEGENDS OF THE JEWS, Louis Ginzberg, The Jewish Publication Society, Philadelphia, 1947.

THE PENTATEUCH, Dr. J. H. Hertz, Editor, Soncino Press, England, 1936.

www.ingramcontent.com/pod-product-compliance
Lightning Source LLC
Chambersburg PA
CBHW030513100426
42813CB00001B/22

* 9 7 8 0 8 2 4 6 0 4 7 5 2 *